Positive Spin

OTHER BOOKS BY JANET E LAPP

Dancing with Tigers
Plant your Feet Firmly in Mid-Air

Positive Spin

**Why you are working harder,
having less fun,
and what you can do about it.**

Janet E Lapp RN PhD

Global Creative Media Inc.
New York Las Vegas

Library of Congress Publisher's Cataloging-In-Publication Data
Lapp, Janet E.

Positive Spin
/ Janet E. Lapp
          p.cm.
      Includes bibliographic references and index.
      ISBN 1-885365-02-0
      1. Organizational change. 2. Conduct of life. 3. Happiness.
          I.Title   II. Title.

BF575.H27 S45 2004
158–dc21

Global Creative Media Inc. is an imprint of Demeter Press

Printing number
10 9 8 7 6 5 4 3

Second printing, February 2004

To brave women and men
everywhere who fight for the truth.

Contents

Positive Spin
By Janet Lapp, Ph.D.

Part I   **The Search for Happiness**
Chapter One   Life, Liberty, and the Purchase
                      of Happiness   13
Chapter Two   Let Freedom Ring   25
Chapter Three   Peace, Order, and Good Government   35

Part II   **The Evidence**
Chapter Four   So If We're So Rich,
                      Why Are We Miserable?   41
Chapter Five   If It Ain't Broke, Don't Break It.
                      Well, It's Broke.   65
Chapter Six   "Maybe If We Moved to California"   81
Chapter Seven   Snow White Was A Snow Job   91
Chapter Eight   War is a Four-Letter Word   103
Chapter Nine   Does Happiness Matter?   113

Part III   **How to Be Happy (no, *really*)**
Chapter Ten   With a Little Help from my Friends   123
Chapter Eleven   Happiness: Flow and Faith   133
Chapter Twelve   Happiness: The Three Actions: 147
Chapter Thirteen   Happiness: The Four Keys: 157
Chapter Fourteen   Ubuntu: A Way of Life, a Solution
                      for our World   173

Appendix   181
Index   197
References   199
Action Notes   221

If there be righteousness in the heart,
  there will be beauty in character.
If there be beauty in character,
  there will be harmony in the home.
If there be harmony in the home,
  there will be order in the nation.
If there be order in the nation,
  there will be peace in the world.
  --CONFUCIUS, Book of Rites

Introduction

*The most perfect society is that whose purpose
is the universal and supreme happiness.
Gottfried Wilhelm Leibniz, On Natural Law, c.1690*

In reflecting upon the incongruence between the philosophy implicated above, and our current political orientation, I began researching the philosophical underpinnings of my adopted country, the United States. I was intrigued especially by what I discovered was the core meaning of Life, Liberty and the Pursuit of Happiness, and how this meaning has been misinterpreted. It is not as much that we have been sold "a pack of lies" as many of the resources below would indicate, but that we have never bothered to examine our true origin, and what our course should be. It is not effective to blame the ruling classes for actions that we have failed to take. Democracy is not a spectator sport; we are not watching a television serial. This stuff is real. We are at war. Poverty and depression are increasing at alarming rates. The middle class (you and me) are being eliminated.

Although 'exposure' material has been dribbling into the mainstream for several years, e.g. Boller's (1996) *Not So!: Popular Myths About America's Past from Columbus to Clinton*, Corn's (1996). *The Lies of George W. Bush: Mastering the Politics of Deception*, and Loewen's (1996) *Lies My Teacher Told Me: Everything Your American History book didn't teach you*, **2003 has been an banner year** with Alterman's (2003) *What Liberal Media? The Truth About Bias and the News*, Ehrman,'s (2003) *Lost Scriptures: Books that did not make it into the New Testament*, Franken's (2003) *Lies and the Lying Liars Who Tell Them: A Fair and Balanced Look at the Right*, Howard's (2003) *White Lies*, Ivins, M. & Dubose, L. (2003). *Bushwhacked: Life in George W. Bush's America* and Krugman's (2003) *The Great Unraveling: Losing Our Way in the New Century.*

Much of the above material suggests that the country is filled with lies and bias, narcissism and greed; and that the ruling classes are feeding us false and misleading information. Although *Positive Spin* agrees with much of the above, it prefers reflection to rancor, suggestion to cynicism. The misinterpretation of the American Founding Fathers' intention *has* led to a country filled with false expectations and unrealistic attitudes toward success and happiness. In our efforts to achieve the impossible American dream, we are exhausting ourselves, ignoring our children, and allowing the ruling classes free reign to do with us whatever they wish. It is as if Disney, the Media, Madison Avenue, the Political Machine and our Major Institutions have created for us a parallel universe, in which our needs can never be met, and wherein the ruling class becomes stronger and we, the passive and manipulated masses, become weaker and weaker. *1984* has arrived.

Vision without action is hallucination; so too, anger without expression is self-destructive. The worst thing that we can do is to use anger to divide ourselves as a nation; that would be exactly what would lead to our destruction.

> "A house divided against itself cannot stand." I believe this government cannot endure permanently half slave and half free. I do not expect the Union to be dissolved–I do not expect the house to fall–but I do expect it will cease to be divided. It will become all one thing, or all the other. Either the opponents of slavery will arrest the further spread of it, and place it where the public mind shall rest in the belief that it is in the course of ultimate extinction; or its advocates will push it forward till it shall become alike lawful in all the States, old as well as new, North as well as South. *Abraham Lincoln, 1858*

Positive Spin is a straightforward, hard-hitting account of where we are now, and what we need to do to join together and turn things around. We still have the power to make a positive and lasting difference in our own lives, in our communities, and in the world at large. This power derives firstly, from knowledge, an awareness of the truth of our current situation, and how futile is our present course. Secondly, our power derives from the concerted and deliberate actions we take each day, as we re-evaluate our thinking, our interactions with others, and the changes needed in our social and political systems.

In *Positive Spin* you will explore the root causes of our current unhappiness, and the research supporting the nature of genuine happiness. Part One examines the true intent of our founding fathers' declaration for the freedom to pursue happiness, and takes a close look at what we hold as most valuable and important in our day to day lives.

Part Two exposes the reality of our situation, including the ills of society, the state of our mental and physical health, and the role that the pursuit of money has played in our relentless pursuit of pleasure. It also discusses how our current global conflict has derived from this same basic irrational foundation to our belief system.

Part Three offers evidence on what does make us happy, and why happiness–in the truest, deepest sense of the word–is worth creating in our lives. It examines the role that the African concept of *Ubuntu* can have in our western lives, how it can eventually lead to world peace, and how we can be part of that creation. *Positive Spin* is not about positive thinking. It is a re-evaluation of evidence, and about the hope and optimism that emanates from knowledge, truth, and right action.

San Diego, California,
February, 2004

Chapter One

Life, Liberty, and the Purchase of Happiness

**Think positively! Create abundance–right here,
right now! Hummer–Out of this World.
Drink Absolut! Buy Prada! Compare *Your*
Wedding to Trista & Ryan's $4 Million
Dream Wedding!**

Although happiness has long been an American obsession, self-help gurus and Madison Avenue advertising have been relentless in their prescription of an array of panaceas that promise ultimate pleasure and self-satisfaction. Our obsessive pursuit of happiness has increased dramatically over the past couple of decades (Easterbrook, 2003; Gallup & Newport, 1990).

Concomitant with the relentless race for 'happiness' over the past 200 years, North America's fixation on sickness and disease has emphasized the diagnosis and treatment of pathology. This preoccupation with disease, and the negativity that it breeds, together with the search-for-love-in-all-the-wrong-places, has led to a Perfect Storm of discontent; a continent

> **This preoccupation with disease, and the negativity that it breeds, together with the search-for-love-in-all-the-wrong-places, has led to a Perfect Storm of discontent.**

filled with angst-ridden people subject to sub-clinical depression (Seligman, 1989; Klerman & Weissman, 1989; Cross-National Collaborative Group, 1992).

Consequently, and understandably, the biggest goals we have in the Western world involve individual choices, rights, and fulfillment. We are occupied with what we can, and cannot, *accomplish* and what we can, and cannot, *acquire*. In our capitalist society, our acquisition of material goods and services, and our fascination with the money that allows us to buy them, represent a socially-sanctioned method of satisfying our appetite for sensory pleasure and fleeting moments of happiness.

The result is ever-increasing greed and materialism that can never be satisfied. We are turning ourselves into commodities. We want to be 'marketable', keep our 'options open', and 'cash in' on what happens to us, especially misfortune. Professional speakers who have suffered and overcome calamities can command higher performance fees. We pursue volunteer work because it looks good on our graduate school resumes. No wonder people are alienated, and no wonder depression is on the rise among young adults (Miller, 2002).

> **The concept of 'pursuing happiness' has been misinterpreted.**

Clearly, the concept of 'pursuing happiness' has been misinterpreted. We are on a collision course with disaster. Unfortunately, although the evidence is all around us, few people are seeing the signs that point to the incredible obstacles we are facing. More importantly, unless we know we have a problem, there is no reason for us to search for a solution or alternate action.

The Problem with Positive Thinking

In *The Positive Thinkers,* Meyer (1988) traced the history of positive thinking through Phineas Quimby, Mary Baker Eddy, Dale Carnegie, Norman Vincent Peale, and Ronald Reagan. The popular psychology of positive thinking flourished among people able to imagine that the only thing wrong with their lives was within their own minds. If they could learn how to manage their thinking, the world would be positive in its response. This world was always North America, of course, and did not include the unfortunates who were born outside our boundaries. God's abundance was somehow meant only for us.

Thus, self-help books promise us success if only we will think positively (Starker, 1989). If our lives are in shambles, we are illiterate, live below the poverty line, and our teenage pregnant daughter is on drugs, there is obviously something wrong with our thinking. We are in 'poverty consciousness' and are not 'manifesting our abundance.'

> **As we manifest our abundance by acquiring more and more worldly goods, our nation is becoming poorer.**

Collectively, we have missed the mark. Yes, we are fortunate to live in privilege, in one of the greatest countries in the world; a country with opportunity–a country with freedom. We have all benefitted from capitalism. My concern is that, as we manifest our abundance by acquiring more and more worldly goods, and carry on our endless pursuit of happiness, our nation is becoming poorer (Pear, 2003). This endless pursuit of happiness and self-knowledge has, paradoxically, made us *less happy.* The pursuit of wealth has not increased our sense of joy and we know scant more today about how to create a happy and successful life than we did decades ago.

Fuzzy Americanisms such as optimism, capitalism, materialism, and individualism have substituted for, and obfuscated, a real understanding of the factors that could increase our real happiness. By our very pursuit of the 'good life,' we may be helping to create the unhappiness and unrest around the globe. Time to grow up.

Fortunately, we have a choice. Left alone on the pinnacle of economic and political leadership, North America (both Bay Street *and* Wall Street) can keep increasing its material wealth while ignoring the human needs of its people and those of the rest of the planet. The February 2003 Survey by the Program on International Policy Attitudes, has shown that Americans are under the impression that as much as 20 percent of the federal budget goes to foreign aid. In truth, the figure is less than one percent, and Canada's record is currently no better. Inevitably, this will lead to increasing selfishness, to alienation between the more and the less fortunate, and eventually to chaos and despair. Already, global dissatisfaction and envy have become alarmingly evident in the current attitude toward American foreign policy.

> **Americans are under the impression that as much as 20 percent of the federal budget goes to foreign aid. In truth, the figure is less than one percent.**

We are long overdue for a drastic course correction. We need to stop in our tracks and reconsider our direction. The task of preventing medical and social ills in this new century, will be to create a science of human strength whose mission is to understand and learn how to foster hope in young people. This is impossible if we stay our current course. To turn things around, we must first re-examine our direction, our pursuits, and our definitions of happiness.

Life, Liberty, and the Pursuit of Happiness

"We hold these truths to be self-evident, that all men are created equal, that they are endowed by their Creator with certain unalienable Rights, that among these are Life, Liberty and the pursuit of Happiness."
The Declaration of Independence

The previous sentence is one of the most popular and frequently quoted statements in the United States' Declaration of Independence. But what did our forefathers have in mind with regard to our right to 'pursue happiness?' Did they mean that every American is free to seek happiness without considering the effects of their actions on themselves or others? When you consider that the men who wrote the Declaration of Independence were in the process of uniting independent states in the spirit of "all for one and one for all," the answer "no," seems obvious. However, many people are living as if the pursuit of individual happiness justifies any and all ill-effects of their choices and actions.

To review the founders' intentions, explained in more depth in the next chapter, consider the widespread philosophies and ideas of five men prior to 1776. David Hume (1711–76), a Scottish philosopher and historian, was a founder of the skeptical, or agnostic, school of philosophy. He felt that the 'pursuit of happiness' was the basis of both individual motivation and social well being. The English philosopher John Locke (1632–1704), one of the pioneers in modern thinking, said, "That we call good which is apt to cause or increase pleasure, or diminish pain" (p. 2), whereas evil is the reverse; it is what causes or increases pain and diminishes pleasure.

> **Many people made the assumption that making more money and having greater control over the material environment would lead to more pleasure and greater happiness.**

The generation of utilitarian philosophers that followed, such as David Hartley (1705–57), Joseph Priestley (1733–1804), and Jeremy Bentham (1748–1832), construed a good society as that which allows the greatest happiness for the greatest number (Bentham, 1789/1970, pp. 64-65). This focus on pleasure or happiness as the touchstone of private and public life was not a concept originated in the 1700's, but rather had already been in the writings of the Greek philosophers. Aristotle noted that although humankind values many things, such as health, fame, and possessions, because we think that they will make us happy, we value happiness for itself. Happiness is the only intrinsic goal that people seek for its own sake, the bottom line of all desire. *It is the interpretation of what happiness is, and how we can achieve it, that has been misinterpreted.*

The idea to include the pursuit of happiness as one of the responsibilities of a just government was enshrined in the Declaration of Independence. Utilitarian philosophy coincided with the start of forward strides in public health and the manufacturing and distribution of goods. Because of this, many people made the assumption that making more money and having greater control over the material environment would lead to more pleasure and greater happiness. The immense self-confidence of the Western technological nations was in large part because of the belief that materialism–the prolongation of a healthy life, the acquisition of wealth, the ownership of consumer goods–would be the road to a happy life.

But the monopoly of materialism as the dominant ideology hasn't made us happier. In fact, in many ways it's actually made us feel empty, frustrated, and exhausted. It amounts to little more than a thoughtless hedonism, a call to do one's thing regardless of consequences, a belief that whatever feels good at the moment must be worth doing.

Are We Happy Yet?

"Happiness isn't something you experience;
it's something you remember."
Oscar Levant (1906 - 1972)

Self-reports from ten years ago indicated that most people felt satisfied with life (Inglehart, 1990; Myers, 1993). In Western Europe and North America, eight of ten rated themselves as more satisfied than dissatisfied. Fewer than one in ten rated themselves as more dissatisfied than satisfied. Likewise, some 75 percent say they have felt 'excited,' 'proud', or 'pleased' at some point during the past few weeks; no more than a third say they have felt lonely, bored, or depressed. Not bad, as far as self-reports go.

These percentages have not changed significantly. In the National Opinion Research Center surveys, three in ten Americans say they are "very happy." Only one in ten say they are "not too happy." The remaining six in ten describe themselves as "pretty happy." Yet, the idea that others are not so happy persists: More than two thirds of a representative sample of Minnesotans rate their "capacity for happiness" in the upper 35 percent "of other people of your age and sex" (Lykken, 1999). We need to believe that we are as happy as, or happier than, other people, although some reports (e.g. Easterbrook, 2003) indicates that we never will.

> **We're supposed to be happy, so we *must* be happy. Have we developed a massive delusional system?**

Depression rates are on the rise. In one multinational assessment of psychiatric disorders, the lifetime rate of depression was nine percent (Cross-National Collaborative Group, 1992), with depression among girls age 14 to 16 peaking at 13.3 percent, the highest in history. At any time, about two percent of people (five million) suffer major depression or bipolar disorder (National Advisory Mental Health Council, 1993) and one in ten adults suffer from mild to moderate depression (Miller, 2002).

Psychiatric Disorders across the Female Reproductive Cycle
Laura J. Miller, M.D. *Annual Review of Psychiatry* 2002

Age	FEMALE	MALE
11	.5%	2.5%
14-16	**13.3%**	2.7%
18-24	6.9%	3.8%
25-44	10.8%	4.8%
45-64	7.8%	3.3%

So, are the people who self-report happiness in denial of their misery? By definition, the final judge of someone's subjective well being is whoever lives inside that person's skin. "If you feel happy," noted Freedman (1978), "you are happy–that's all we mean by the term." However, the data are misleading. Quite simply, in America, the socially appropriate response to the question "Are you happy?" is "yes." We're supposed to be happy, so we must be happy. Have we developed a massive delusional system based on the premise that "This is the road to happiness as I was taught by my political system and the current ruling class, the media. If I am on this road, I must be happy." It is just too incongruous for us to hold two incompatible beliefs; "I am on the road, and I am not happy."

Some people really *are* happy; supposedly, people such as the Dalai Llama, and Elie Weisel. Elie Weisel? Weisel was born in Transylvania in 1928, the only son of four children in a Hassidic Jewish community. In 1944, at age 15, he and his family were sent to Auschwitz. Separated from his mother and younger sister, he remained with his father, who died in the last months of the war. He never saw his mother and sister again. After the war, Weisel spent a few years in a French orphanage and in 1948, began to study literature, philosophy and psychology at the Sorbonne, publishing *Night* in 1958. Weisel wrote 35 additional works about Judaism, the Holocaust and the fight for morality among the races. In 1985, Weisel was awarded the Congressional Gold Medal of Achievement and a year later, the Nobel Peace Prize. Weisel has dedicated his life to helping us remember who we are. When you are near him, you *know* his happiness, and it is life-changing.

> *"What is man? Hope turned to dust. No. What is man? Dust turned to hope."*
> **Elie Weisel**

Perhaps he is different. Maybe they have something we don't, these happy people. We have learned, for example, that certain traits and temperaments predispose a person to experience happiness. Some of these traits, such as anxiety levels, are genetically influenced (Weinberger (2002)[1] but, like cholesterol levels, happiness can be genetically influenced, but not genetically *fixed*. That means that regardless of our genes, we have the capacity to increase our level of happiness by taking a proactive stance. If Elie Weisel can be happy, so can we.

> **If people expect their lives to be filled with joy and ecstasy, whether it be through their career or a love relationship, they are likely to be disappointed.**

So, what is 'happy'? Although most people report being "above neutral" in mood most of the time (Diener & Diener, 1996), intense positive moments are rare even among the happiest individuals (Diener et al., 1991). In other words, true moments of joy and bliss are few and far between.

---

[1] **Anxiety and Genetics**

Reporting in *Science*, Weinberger (2002) stated that each person carries two copies of the gene in question, called SLC6A4, one copy from each parent. The proposed gene comes in two forms, 'long' and 'short,' the short one showing up more often in anxiety. Therefore, any individual can get two copies of the long version, two of the short, or one of each. About 40 percent of the genes in the population are short. Earlier studies had shown that people with one or two copies of the short version were more prone to anxiety than those with two longs.

The gene influences the way the brain processes serotonin, which has been connected to moods and mood disorders. Prozac and other drugs in its family work by altering the balance of serotonin in the brain. The gene is critical for serotonin being taken up into cells. The long version creates a longer protein that works more efficiently. Anxiety is a complicated, multidimensional characteristic of human experience and cannot be predicted by the form of a single gene. The influence of the gene is subtle; those with one or two shorts have only a *slightly* higher risk of anxiety disorders, since this gene is just one of many factors, both inherited and environmental, at work.

Rather than reporting one 'high' after another, happy people report mild-to-moderate pleasant emotions most of the time. 'Most of the time' means when they alone, and with others, and when they are working, and at leisure. If people expect their lives to be filled with joy and ecstasy, whether it be through their career or a love relationship, they are likely to be disappointed. Even worse, they may move to the next relationship or job, seeking intense levels of happiness, which, in fact, are rarely long lasting, and are not necessary for happiness. Intense experiences are not the cornerstone of a happy life. Furthermore, according to some theories of adaptation, such as that of Parducci (1995), highly pleasurable experiences may have the disadvantage of serving as a contrast point against which to compare other positive experiences, thus making the mild events less pleasurable.

SUMMARY

Although happiness has long been an American obsession, self-help gurus and the media have been relentless in their positive spin on life. Our obsessive pursuit of happiness has increased dramatically over the past couple of decades.

Concomitant with the relentless race for 'happiness' over the past 200 years, North America's fixation on sickness and disease has emphasized the diagnosis and treatment of pathology.

This preoccupation with disease, and the negativity that it breeds, together with the search-for-love-in-all-the-wrong-places, has led to a Perfect Storm of discontent.

A Positive Spin

ACTION

a) If positive thinking is not enough, what is? Check into Chapter 10 for the foundation of happiness: Flow and Faith.

b) If you desire true happiness, fulfilling only your own dreams will not get you there; check into Chapters 12-14 to find out what else is needed. And sheer materialism–forget it, it's actually making you miserable.

c) On a personal satisfaction scale of 1-10, don't expect or wish for a 9 or 10 (because it isn't possible, and will lead to all sorts of problems). Instead, aim for a reasonable 6-8 satisfaction level most of the time. Every so often, a 9-10 will surprise you, and expect 4-5 from time to time.

In Chapter Two, look for more interpretation of the Positive Spin that has been cast for us.

Chapter Two
Let Freedom Ring

*"If liberty and equality, as is thought by some, are chiefly to be
found in democracy, they will be best attained when all persons
alike share in the government to the utmost."*
Aristotle, Politics

Although John Locke has been credited with influencing the intention and creation of the Declaration of Independence, the American Revolution was actually a battle *against* Locke's philosophy and the English utilitarians.

It was *The Law of Nations* by the 18th century jurist, Emmerich de Vattel, which guided the United States as the world's first constitutional republic. From this, America's founders learned Leibnizian natural law, which became the basis for the American System. The myth that the founding of the American Republic was based on the philosophy of John Locke was maintained only because the history of Leibniz's influence was suppressed. This led to both our greatness, and to our greatest dilemma.

Why is this important? Vattel showed the consistency of Christian charity with natural law. He taught that Christ's instruction, "Love your enemies," was proven by natural law (Vattel, 1762). *The Law of Nations*, published in 1758, was widely read in the American Colonies, and was the most influential book on the law of nations for 125 years following its publication, until it was suppressed.

> **Consequently, the vast majority of Americans today think of freedom as the equivalent of "doing your own thing."**

Why suppressed? The financial bosses of the 18th century, the Venetian Party headquartered in England, planned to wipe out the modern nation-state. They launched the Enlightenment to spread the ideology that man was no more than a hedonistic animal controlled by his sensual urges. By destroying the ability of men to think and act like citizens, they aimed to destroy the basis for the existence of the nation-state as an opponent to their complete control of human society. These theories of the Enlightenment became the basis for Thomas Hobbes (1588–1679), an English political theorist and John Locke, who also assumed that human hedonistic desires were self-evident, and built society from that basic faulty premise. Hobbes is well known for his bestial portrayal of human nature. John Locke, portrayed as the source of the ideas of freedom and government, which motivated the founding fathers, was actually no further ahead in his thinking than Hobbes.

> **By destroying the ability of men to think and act like citizens, they aimed to destroy the basis for the existence of the nation-state as an opponent to their complete control of human society.**

Locke wrote that we are born as blank slates, and believed that "thinking is only sense perception, and that the mind lacks the power to invent or frame one new simple idea" (Locke, ref. 1959). "The knowledge of the existence of any other thing, we can have only by sensation: for there being no necessary connection of real existence with any idea a man hath in his memory; but only when, by actual operating upon him, it makes itself perceived by him." We shall see in Chapter Five how this control is manipulated by the ruling classes and how the media absolutely requires us to ascribe to the blank slate theory.

"As to myself, I think God has given me assurance enough of the existence of things without me: since by their different application, I can produce in myself both pleasure and pain, which is one great concernment of my present state" (Locke, ref. 1959).

From this base view–that the human mind consisted of only sense certainty, pleasure and pain–Locke developed the following national theory:

Man originally existed in a State of Nature of complete liberty. If he was attacked by another, he was justified in seeking retribution. It is not difficult to see how this fundamental atttributional error has contributed to the irrational behavior of 'preventive' assaults on other countries.

> **Man originally existed in a State of Nature of complete liberty. If he was attacked by another, he was justified in seeking retribution.**

The state came to be an umpire, justified in setting rules for the correct amount of 'just retribution.' Through this thinking, the commonwealth was able to set punishments and to defend itself against outsiders. Locke's conception of freedom was no more than the right of each man to follow his hedonistic instincts in all things. Consistent with these views, in Locke's 1669 'Fundamental Constitution for the Government of Carolina,' he established a system of both Black and White slavery.

An examination of Locke's influence on Thomas Jefferson refutes the myth that Locke's theories formed the theoretical underpinning behind the American Republic. Jefferson made it clear that, had Locke's philosophy been the inspiration for the American

Revolution, the United States would never have become the world's leading nation and industrial power. Jefferson claimed that the three greatest men in history were the British empiricists Francis Bacon, John Locke, and Isaac Newton (Jefferson, 1789, cited in Peterson (ed.), 1984) and adopted their outlook that empirical evidence is the basis for all knowledge:

> *"I feel, therefore I exist. I feel bodies, which are not myself:*
> *there are other existences then. I call them matter. I feel them*
> *changing place. This gives me motion. Where there is an*
> *absence of matter, I call it void, or nothing, or immaterial space.*
> *On the basis of sensation, of matter and motion, we may erect*
> *the fabric of all the certainties we can have or need."*
> *(Locke, Letter to John Adams, 1820, cited in Merrill, 1984)*

Having denied that human nature is creative reason, Jefferson saw both society and economics based on fixed relationships. He rejected national economic development through the increase of the productive powers of labor, and instead accepted Adam Smith's free trade doctrines. Jefferson saw slavery as appropriate for Blacks, whom he considered as inherently inferior. Jefferson was opposed to the development of American industry and described the growth of cities in America as "a canker which soon eats to the heart of its laws and constitution." He fought to keep the nation as a feudal plantation. Yet, his image is on the American nickel and a commemorative silver dollar. Each year, thousands of people explore, *sans reflection*, the house, gardens, and plantations of Monticello, Jefferson's mountaintop home. The third American president is also one of the four faces carved into the stone of Mount Rushmore. Although we understand all behaviors in their historical and social context, and are tolerant of human err, we also are aware of the need for *je me souviens,* or remembering the truth of our past.

> *"It is in justice that the ordering*
> *of society is centered."*
> *Aristotle*

In some ways, Jefferson and Leibniz were polar opposites. For example, Leibniz developed a science of the mind, which was congruent with human nature as creative reason. For humanity to make fundamental changes in its methods of existence, "men must be capable of creative reason, instead of merely taking in sensual impressions and acting on instincts." Leibniz described how the mind recognizes contradictions in sensual impressions and generates Platonic ideas, which are "by far to be preferred to the blank tablets of Aristotle, Locke, and the other recent exoteric philosophers" (cited in Loemker, 1989, pp. 592-95).

> *"The stupid neither forgive nor forget; the naive forgive and forget; the wise forgive but do not forget."*
> *Thomas Szasz*

Leibniz demonstrated how the principles of science and law are also "not derived from sense, but from a clear and distinct intuition, which Plato called an idea" (cited in Loemker, 1989, p. 133). Plato discussed, in the Republic, how sense impressions do not provoke thought, because the judgment of them by sensation seems adequate, while others always invite the intellect to reflection, because the senses give the mind contrary perceptions. "These sense impressions force the mind to conceptualize an explanation, which is intelligible rather than visible."

29

"To give a satisfactory decision as to the truth it is necessary to be rather an arbitrator than a party to the dispute."
Aristotle

Leibniz and Locke also differed in their views of the nature of God. Leibniz's God is the Creator, who is able to transform the universe to higher levels, reflected in the transformation of human society. "What is true of books, is also true of the different states of the world; every subsequent state is somehow copied from the preceding one–although according to certain laws of change" (cited in Loemker, 1989, p. 316).

> **So we aspire to the pinnacle of our Horatio Alger dreams, whilst doomed unknowingly into a caste system of which we are not aware.**

Locke was unable to view the universe as evolving; rather seeing God as trapped in a set of fixed rules. Since not even God could change these laws, humanity must live in a trapped universe. Locke developed a system of law and a model of society, in which people are trapped in categories, much like a caste system. Leibniz understood that the idea of man living in accordance with natural law means ordering society according to the powers of creative reason, which makes man in the image of God. So we aspire to the pinnacle of our Horatio Alger dreams, whilst doomed unknowingly, into a base caste system of which we have no awareness.

Leibniz confirmed the two traditional notions of right that were originally codified by Aristotle. The higher of these two, Leibniz called equity. This included distributive justice, or the precept of the law that commands us to give each one what he merits or deserves. The lower was the strict right of commutative justice that no one is to be injured. "The strict right avoids misery where-as the next higher right, equity, tends toward happiness, but only such as fall within this mortality" (cited in Loemker, 1989, pp. 421-444).

It is the responsibility of the state, to make laws that transform the moral claims of equity, such as the obligation to take care of the sick, investigate legal claims, and thereby assure the happiness of the people. The transformation from the middle to the highest level, is the difference between desiring good of others for our own benefit, and desiring good of others because it is our own good. On this level, humans determine the justice of their acts, by weighing their consequences against the past, present, and future.

> **The transformation from the middle to the highest level, is the difference between desiring good of others for our own benefit, and desiring good of others because it is our own good.**

However, Leibniz felt that the "clear comprehension of the mind" that was needed to understand justice on its highest level, is achieved by few, and the hope for improvement for humanity rests on those great men.

For Leibniz, true happiness is found by people helping other people. Consider the following words of Leibniz and Vattel.

"Happiness is the point where center all those duties which individuals and nations owe to themselves; and this is the great end of the law of nature. The desire of happiness is the powerful spring that puts man in motion: felicity is the end they all have in view, and it ought to be the grand object of the public will.

To succeed in this, it is necessary to instruct the people to seek
felicity where it is to be found; that is, in their own perfection."
(Leibniz, cited in Loemker, 1989, p. 326)

Through education and developing technology and science, he worked to improve the power of labor so the population could be lifted out of backwardness. The 1776 Declaration of Independence and 1789 Federal Constitution were premised on the philosophy of Leibniz. Natural law must be grounded in the requirements for successful human survival. In other words, for a society to survive, it must generate a sufficient level of physical production to meet its current needs, and to produce a surplus for upgrading its productive powers. The intellect of a society's members and a minimal standard of demographics and consumption determine the level of that society's potential physical productivity. No society has ever survived by remaining in a steady state.

"The only stable state is the one in which
all men are equal before the law."
Aristotle

The successful existence of the human species requires that it develop within its people, the capability to make the scientific discoveries necessary to achieve progress. The quality of mind required for mankind to make necessary, successive scientific discoveries, however, is completely different from the view presented by Locke–that knowledge is nothing more than a collection of sense impressions. Most, if not all, of psychological thought dating back to the American philosopher and psychologist, William James (1842–1910), is based on empirical laws, and as such is rooted in Lockian thought. As such, we have been trapped in empiricism; if we cannot measure it, it cannot exist.

SUMMARY

1. Freedom means responsibility for others.

2. Americans seem to be unaware that there once was an "American System." Most still believe that the American Constitution developed from John Locke's Social Contract. Consequently, the vast majority of Americans today think of freedom as the equivalent of "doing your own thing." But this misinterpretation couldn't be further from the truth.

ACTION

1. Can you see how, if Leibniz' ideas were truly recognized as our founding belief system, that we might presently be at peace?

2. Can you see how this belief system fundamentally reflects the beliefs of all natural healers, wise sages, and native peoples around the globe, and it is in the ignoring of it that we are leading ourselves into chaos and disharmony?

In Chapter Three, we explore the properties of good government, applicable to not only our political system, but to our corporate world as well.

Chapter Three
Peace, Order, and Good Government

Our ability to make creative discoveries depends on *agape*, or the emotion associated with creativity. Through such discoveries, we contribute to the perfection of all humanity. Plato associated *agape* with the love of truth and the love of justice. St. Paul extended that definition to include the love of mankind and God. This emotion of love contrasts with eros, or a fixation on sensual pleasure.

> *"The first general law that we discover in the very object*
> *of the society of nations, is that each individual nation is*
> *bound to contribute every thing in her power to the*
> *happiness and perfection of all the others."*
> *Emmerich de Vattel, The Law of Nations, 1758*

Therefore, in order for a society to survive and evolve, its members must share a vested interest in improving the current conditions for everyone. By making that the common goal, you establish an environment in which more happiness is possible. In the words of Leibniz, "The most perfect society is that whose purpose is the universal and supreme happiness." By making the happiness of *all* paramount, we often receive the reward of greater individual happiness. This is the "pursuit of happiness" that the forefathers intended when they scribed these words in the opening of the *Declaration of Independence*, and in the "General Welfare" clause in the Preamble to the U.S. Constitution.

Since men can live "consonant to their nature" only by the development of their creative potential through collaboration with others, a society which does not develop the emotion of *agape* in its members, is self-destructive.

> **No individual can live happily or improve his nature without the assistance of others.**

"Humans are so formed by nature that they cannot supply all their own wants, but need assistance of their fellow-creatures. No individual can live happily or improve his nature without the assistance of others. Because nature has thus formed the human condition, it is proof of nature's intention that all humans should communicate with, and mutually aid and assist each other. The general law of a natural society is that each individual should do for the others everything which their necessities require, and which he can perform without neglecting the duty that he owes to himself: a law which all men must observe in order to live in a manner consonant to their nature, and conformable to the views of their common Creator, a law which our own safety, our happiness, our dearest interests, ought to render sacred to every one of us" (Wolff, 1934).

Vattel (cited in Chitty, 1857) writes,

> "It is easy to conceive what exalted felicity the world would enjoy, were all men willing to observe the rule that we have just laid down. On the contrary, **if each man wholly and immediately directs all his thoughts to his own interest, if he does nothing for the sake of other men, the whole human race together will be immersed in the deepest wretchedness.** Let us

> therefore endeavor to promote the general happi-
> ness of mankind: all mankind, in return, will
> endeavor to promote ours, and thus we shall
> establish our felicity on the most solid founda-
> tions" (Vattel, Preliminaries, Sec. 10).

Vattel insisted that when men join in a nation, they must still fulfill their duties toward the rest of mankind. He writes: "That society, considered as a moral person, since possessed of an understanding, volition, and strength peculiar to itself, is therefore
obliged to live on the same terms with other societies or states, as
individual man was obliged, before those establishments, to live
with other men ... the object of the great society established by
nature between all nations is also the interchange of mutual assistance for their own improvement, and that of their condition"
(Vattel, Preliminaries, Sec. 11-12).

From this, Vattel arrives at two general laws of relations
between nations:

1. **The first general law is that each individual nation is bound
to contribute every thing in her power to the happiness and
perfection of all the others.** (Preliminaries, Sec. 13)

> *"No nation ever supports values that transcend its life*
> *if they are diametrically opposed to the preservation of its life.*
> *Nations can and do support higher values than their own*
> *if there is a coincidence between the higher values*
> *and the impulse of survival."*
> *Reinhold Niebuhr*
> *Radical Religion, Fall, 1939,*
> *in Love and Justice, p. 79.*

2. The second general law of relations between nations is the **sovereignty of all nations**: "Each nation should be left in the peaceable enjoyment of that liberty which she inherits from nature."

> The ordering principle governing relations between nations, must be each nation contributing everything in its power to the perfection and happiness of other nations.

This is derived from natural law, since nations, like individuals, are naturally free and independent of each other, regardless of the size or strength of the nation. "A dwarf is as much a man as a giant; a small republic is not less a sovereign state than the most powerful kingdom."

With these two laws as our guides, we decide on foreign policy, intervention, and prevention. Our corporations can be modeled upon these laws. Are we on course?

A Nation Considered in its Relation to Others

"It is impossible that nations should mutually discharge all these several duties if they do not love each other."

Vattel asserted that the ordering principle governing relations between nations, must be each nation contributing everything in its power to the perfection and happiness of other nations. He writes:

> "How happy would mankind be, were these amiable precepts of nature everywhere observed! Nations would communicate to each other their products and their knowledge; a profound peace would prevail all over the earth, and enrich it with its invaluable fruits; industry, the sciences, and the arts would be employed in promoting our

happiness, no less than in relieving our wants; violent methods of deciding contests would be no more heard of; all differences would be terminated by moderation, justice and equity; the world would have the appearance of a large republic; men would live everywhere like brothers, and each individual be a citizen of the universe. That this idea should be but a delightful dream! Yet it flows from the nature and essence of man" (Book II, Chap. I, Sec. 16).

In many ways, we are currently living in conflict with the natural essence of man by putting individual happiness before universal happiness. We are also forgetting that the declaration of independence affirms the "pursuit" of happiness, not the "achievement" of happiness. And in this, we can find some valuable clues for true happiness, individually, in our families and workplaces, and for the world.

SUMMARY

In order for a society to survive and evolve, its members must share a vested interest in improving the current conditions for everyone. By making that the common goal, we establish an environment in which more happiness is possible.

ACTION

The next time you make a decision in your relationship, your work unit, or in your community, remember that laws for happiness and order have been laid down; do what is right for the whole. In the next chapter, we'll consider the consequences of a misdirected interpretation of the founding fathers, and why winning the lottery *really* won't help.

Chapter Four
So If We're So Rich, How Come We're Miserable?

"Our visions begin with our desires."
Audre Lorde

Even if you do accept John Locke's views as the philosophical underpinning of our country's thought, consider Locke's warning about pursuing happiness with care. The importance of distinguishing real from imaginary happiness, is still salient. When we find few meaningful opportunities for action in the environment, we resort to finding 'happiness' in activities that are destructive, addictive, or at the very least, wasteful. Juvenile crime is caused, in part, by the boredom or frustration that results when other opportunities are blocked. Vandalism, gang fights, promiscuous sex, and experimenting with drugs have never led to happiness, and escalate quickly. One can never get enough of what one doesn't need. So we're richer, and we're happier, right?

We seem to have a need to think that we are living good lives. This subjective definition of quality of life is democratic in that it grants each of us the right to decide whether our life is worthwhile. It is this approach to defining the good life that has come to be called 'subjective well being' or 'happiness.'[2] Although subjective well-being appears to be stable over time, it may be based on a faulty premise. A

> **One can never get enough of what one doesn't need.**

concept of 'objective happiness,' distinct from 'subjective well-being,' is preferred because we do not know how happy we are. Our theories about what would make us happy are generally inac-

41

curate, affected by what Kahneman terms a 'focusing illusion' (Kahneman, 2001). This means that we are comparing ourselves with others on a continual moving map of moment-to-moment self-evaluation. This map is based on cultural values, changes with changing trends and societal standards, and it is this moving evaluation that determines our happiness. This becomes important later, as we examine the role of the media in social comparison.

Maybe It Will Get Better

Will we get happen as we age? Some researchers have found *no* time of life happier or more satisfying than any other time. This finding was the result of surveys of 170,000 adults in 16 countries (Inglehart, 1990), surveys of 18,000 university students in 39 countries (Michalos, 1991), and a meta-analysis of 146 other studies (Haring, Stock, & Okun, 1984, Myers & Diener, 1995). So, you're about as happy now as you're going to get.

---

[2]How is happiness measured? A variety of self-report measures of happiness have been used, the assumption being that happiness is a subjective phenomenon, for which the final judge should be "whoever lives inside a person's skin" (Myers & Diener, 1995, p. 11). Most of these measures have adequate psychometric properties such that the associations between happiness and other variables usually cannot be accounted for by transient mood (Diener et al., 1999). Happiness or subjective well being, appears to be relatively stable over time and consistent across situations (Sandvik, Diener, & Seidlitz, 1993). Data from 916 surveys of 1.1 million people in 45 nations recalibrated subjective well being onto a 0-to-10 scale (where 0 is the low extreme–very unhappy or completely dissatisfied with life, 5 is neutral, and 10 is the high extreme) (Myers & Diener, 1996). Diener and his colleagues use the Subjective Well-Being Scale (SWLS), a 5-item instrument designed to measure global cognitive judgments of one's life. The scale can be used without charge and without permission by all professionals (researchers and practitioners), takes about a minute to complete, and is in the public domain. The scale is contained in the Appendix of this book, and a description of psychometric properties of the scale can be found in Pavot and Diener's 1993 article in *Psychological Assessment*.

According to these researchers, emotionality changes with maturity, and the predictors of happiness change. For example, later in life, satisfaction with social relations and health become more important. Despite gender gaps in happiness, in that men more often act antisocial or become alcoholic when unhappy, and women more often ruminate and get depressed or anxious, men

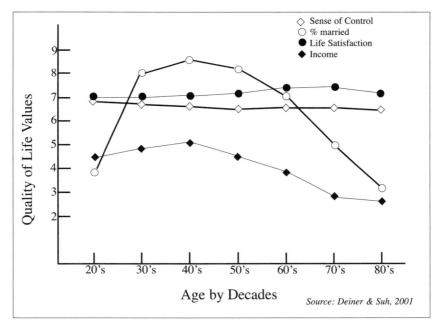

Source: Deiner & Suh, 2001

and women are equally likely to declare themselves "very happy" and "satisfied" with their lives. The Figure above shows the level of well-being variables across different age groups in an international sample, including more than 60,000 adults across 43 nations (Diener & Suh, 2001). Objective resources, such as income and marriage percentage, decline considerably with increasing age. These researchers found that despite the losses in objective resources, elderly people experience *more* satisfactions with their life overall than younger adults. The most probably explanation for this counterintuitive result is that older people adjust their expectations and goals according to the constraints of their situation. Thus, expectations and attributions seem to form a large component of the experience of happiness.

> *"Education is the best provision for the journey to old age."*
> *Aristotle*

The Good Old Days

Are we happier now than in 1940, when two out of five homes lacked a shower or bathtub, heat often meant shoveling coal or wood into a basement furnace, and 35 percent of homes had no indoor toilet? Some of our parents never owned a house, played golf, traveled out of the country, or had a credit card. Some of them received a 'revolving' charge card, but didn't use it because they saved for major purchases with real money and squirreled away their Canadian Tire Cash Bonus money for those extra splurges. I had a one-speed bicycle that weighed over 50 pounds and wore pant leg clips because my bike didn't have chain guards. We used hand signals on our bikes, and our parents' cars didn't have turn signals either.

We didn't have a television set in our house until I was 12. It was black and white, but Dad bought a piece of colored plastic to cover the screen. The top third was blue, like the sky, and the bottom third was green, like grass. The middle third was red. Some people had a transparent magnifying sheet taped to the front of the TV to make the picture look larger.

Heaven forbid, not only did I not have a MP3 player, PlayStation II or even a computer in my room, I never even had a telephone! In fact, the only phone in the house was in the hall, on a party line. Before you could dial, you had to listen and make sure no one was already using the line. Then you gave the operator your number (525-J was ours), and you magically were connected. Well, some of the time.

We were embarrassed when movie stars kissed on the screen. We passed *Peyton Place* to each other under our school desks, highlighting the references to passionate scenes, that would be PG-13 today. There was no fast food. Mom got up at 4:30 a.m. to start the washing, in the old agitator washer and the wringer dryer that we tried to stick our arms through. The clothes were hung outside in the summer and in the basement in the winter, and mom shook water from a bottle to dampen the clothes for pressing because there were no steam irons. Headlight dimmer switches were controlled by a little button on the floor of the car. We had an icebox rather than a refrigerator, and the ice truck came by two or three times a week, the driver giving us big handfuls of sawdust and ice chips.

Was the world of candy cigarettes, coca-cola bottles, coffee shops with vinyl benches and table jukeboxes, home milk delivery in glass bottles with cardboard stoppers, newsreels instead of previews before the movie, Howdy Doody, Hopalong Cassidy, 78-45-33 RPM records, Stereo Hi-Fi's, metal ice trays with levers, mimeograph paper, and roller skate keys any happier? Well, humans adapt quickly to their circumstances, putting us on a 'hedonic treadmill' (Diener, Suh, Lucas, & Smith, 1999, p. 286). Americans today have more cars, color TVs, computers, and brand-name clothes than they did several decades ago, but Americans are no happier now than they were then (Myers & Diener, 1995). We had fewer choices, fewer comparisons, but most importantly, we had hope that things would always get better. Now we sense that they might not.

> **We are no happier now than we were then. We had fewer choices, fewer comparisons, but we had hope that things would get better.**

"If a man takes no thought about what is distant, he will find sorrow near at hand."
Confucius, The Confucian Analects

The Rising Tide

In 1957, economist John Galbraith described the United States as 'The Affluent Society.' At that time, Americans' per person income, expressed in today's dollars, was about $9,000. The U.S. Census Bureaus reported a median 2001 income of $42,228. Compared with 1957, controlling for cost of living, we should be five times more affluent than we were then. Although income disparity has increased between the wealthy and poor, the rising tide has lifted most boats. We own twice as many cars per person, dine out more than twice as often, and enjoy microwave ovens, big-screen color TVs, and home computers. From 1960 to 2004, the percentage of homes with dishwashers increased from seven percent to 50 percent, clothes dryers increased from 20 percent to 71 percent, and air conditioning increased from 15 percent to 73 percent.

So, believing that it is "very important" to be very well off financially, and having seen their affluence increase over four decades, are Americans now happier? Again, they are not. The number of people reporting themselves "very happy" has declined between 1957 and 1998, from 35 percent to 33 percent: We are twice as rich and no happier. Meanwhile, the divorce rate has doubled and teen suicide has tripled. Reported violent crime nearly quadrupled. Depression rates have soared, especially among teens and young adults (Seligman, 1989; Klerman & Weissman, 1989; Cross-National Collaborative Group, 1992).

Compared with their grandparents, today's young adults have grown up with much more affluence, slightly less happiness, and much greater risk of depression and assorted social pathologies. Myers (2001) calls this conjunction of material prosperity and social recession the 'American Paradox.' The more people strive for extrinsic goals such as money, the more numerous their problems and the less robust their well-being (Kasser & Ryan, 1996).

> **Our becoming much better off over the last four decades has not been accompanied by increased subjective well being.**

Easterbrook (2003) has termed these various anxieties of our day as *Catalog-Induced*, whereby we are able to evaluate our paltry digs with the billionaires on 'Lifestyles;' *Collapse Anxiety*, in that we fear the economy will collapse and our natural resources will run out; *Abundance Denial* in that we think more money is needed before we can term ourselves well-off, and so on.

Our becoming much better off over the last four decades has not been accompanied by increased subjective well being. Easterlin (1995) has shown that, in Britain, increases in the percentages of households with cars, central heating, and telephones have not been accompanied by increased happiness. So far as happiness goes, it is not "the economy, stupid." Economic growth in affluent countries has provided no apparent boost to human morale.

Some research has found that most people judge their well-being by the possibilities for improvement in the coming years (Kahneman 2001). The post-war afterglow of the 1950's were filled with high expectations for a better future. Now that 'we have it all', there is no place to go. This realization, coupled with the impending collapse of our Medicare system and our pension plans, has led to a head-on collision with reality.

Happiness Has a Price, But We Can't Buy it

Everyone who is working for work's sake, with little real reward or possibility of obtaining meaningful benefits for their long work hours, are simply too exhausted to take advantage of the benefits.

"It is pretty hard to tell what does bring happiness; poverty and wealth have both failed."
Kin Hubbard (1868 - 1930)

Higher incomes can increase happiness to the extent that they allow the 'earners' to engage in more rewarding activities. Although increasing productivity is a goal of most businesses, it will decrease individual happiness if it demands long hours of tedious work, creates high levels of stress, and/or provides little leisure time. The current productivity thrust in North America might be creating a generation of workers with massive serotonin depletion.[3] Included in this group is everyone who is working for work's sake, with little real reward or possibility of obtaining meaningful benefits for their long work hours. We're simply too exhausted to take advantage of these benefits.

"Would a little more money make you a little happier?

Asked how satisfied they were with 13 aspects of their lives, including friends, house, and schooling, Americans expressed the least satisfaction with "the amount of money you have to live on" (Roper Organization, 1984). What would improve their quality of life? "More money" was the most frequent response to a University of Michigan national survey (Campbell, 1981, p. 41), and the more the better. In one Gallup Poll (Gallup & Newport, 1990), one in two women, two in three men, and four in five people earning more than $75,000 reported they would like to be rich. Thus, the modern American dream seems to have become life, liberty, and the purchase of happiness. Although most realize that the seemingly happy lifestyle of the rich and famous is beyond their reach, they do imagine "the good life" that might become possible when they achieve greater wealth.

According to the annual UCLA and American Council on Education survey of nearly 250,000 students entering college, those agreeing that a "very important" reason for attending college was "to make more money," rose from one in two in 1971, to three in four in 1998 (Sax, Astin, Kom, & Mahoney, 1998). The proportion who consider it "very important or essential" that they

---

[3]**Serotonin Depletion**

The serotoninergic system modulates mood, emotion, sleep and appetite. Decreased serotoninergic neurotransmission has been proposed to play a key role in depression. The concentration of synaptic serotonin is controlled by its reuptake into the pre-synaptic terminal and, thus, drugs blocking serotonin transport have been successfully used for the treatment of depression. Popular books have been written on factors that increase and decrease serotonin levels e.g. Hart (1996).

become "very well off financially" rose from 39 percent in 1970 to 74 percent in 1998. Among 19 listed objectives, money was first, outranking "developing a meaningful philosophy of life," "becoming an authority in my field," "helping others in difficulty," and "raising a family."

The Sloan Foundation longitudinal studies of 1,000 American adolescents found that the higher the material well being, the lower the subjective well-being. Happiness of teenagers shows a significant inverse relationship to the social class of the community in which teens live, to their parents' level of education, and to their parents' occupational status. Children of the lowest socioeconomic strata report the highest happiness, and upper middle-class children generally report the least happiness. Despite this, most people still believe that their problems would be resolved if they only had more money. In a survey conducted at the University of Michigan, when people were asked what would improve the quality of their lives, the first answer was "more money" (Campbell, 1981).

> **Thus, the modern American dream seems to have become life, liberty, and the purchase of happiness.**

Would we be happier if we traded in our 1997 Toyota Camry for a 2004 Turbo Porsche, our three-bedroom suburban tract home for a Caribbean villa? Our advertisers are convincing. "Whoever said money can't buy happiness isn't spending it right," proclaimed a Lexus ad.

However, as reported in the Forbes 100 Wealthiest Americans Report, this group of wealthy people rated themselves to be only slightly happier than the average American. Some reported that they were unhappy (Diener, Horwitz, and Emmons, 1985). One very wealthy man could never remember being happy. One woman reported that money could not undo misery caused by her children's problems.

> ***When sailing on the Titanic,***
> ***even first class cannot***
> ***get you where you want to go.***

"If Only I Could Win the Lottery"

Good and bad events such a pay hike or being turned down for a promotion, do temporarily influence our moods, and people will often seize on such short-run influences to explain their happiness. Yet, the emotional impact of significant events and circumstances soon dissipates (Gilbert, Pinel, Wilson, Blumberg, & Wheatley, 1998).

> **Children of the lowest socioeconomic strata report the highest happiness, and upper middle-class children generally report the least happiness.**

After following a group of lottery winners, Brickman, Coates, and Janoff-Bulman (1978) concluded that, despite their sudden increase in wealth, the winners' happiness was unchanged. Reports of lottery winners suggest that individuals quickly adjust to their new riches, and may be no happier than they were before (some even report increased conflicts with others). On July 9, 2003, William and Claudia Walkenbach of Missouri and Scott and Marian Calligan from Pennsylvania each collected $73,641,790.05. On December 25, 2002, Andrew J. Whittaker Jr. from West Virginia won

$170,505,876.33 from the $314 million Powerball. Envious? Hold on. As we mentioned above, lottery winners do gain a temporary jolt from their winnings (Argyle, 1986; Brickman, Coates, & Janoff-Bulman, 1978). However, although the winners above were delighted to have won, the euphoria quickly faded.

> **Reports of lottery winners suggest that individuals quickly adjust to their new riches, and may be no happier than they were before.**

Thus, happiness may track modern manifestations of ancestral signals of evolutionary fitness (Ketelaar, 1995), but people adjust quickly to any gains they experience, creating the hedonic treadmill where apparent increments in rewards fail to produce sustained increments in personal happiness.

If economic growth in the wealthiest societies increases happiness at all, it increases it only to the extent that:

1) It rewards work activities in pursuit of meaningful goals.
2) Quality of work life is at least as important to happiness as income.
3) Policies foster close relationships and meaningful activities, which are more successful at enhancing happiness, than policies designed only to improve efficiency.

The Rich Get Richer, But They Don't Get Happier[4]

If we work toward a higher level of affluence, thinking that it will make us happy, we find that on reaching it, we become quickly habituated. At that point, we start to look longingly for the next level of income or property. In a 1987 *Chicago Tribune* poll, those who earned less than $30,000 a year said that $50,000 would fulfill their dreams, whereas those with yearly incomes of over $100,000 said they would need $250,000 to be satisfied (Pay Nags, 1987; 'Rich Think Big,' also see Myers, 1993, p. 57). Goals keep getting pushed upward as soon as a lower level is reached. It is not the objective size of the reward but its difference from one's 'adaptation level' that provides subjective value.

Those whose incomes have increased over the previous decade are not happier than those whose income has *not* increased (Diener, Sandvik, Seidlitz, & Diener, 1993). Brickman and Campbell (1971) suggested that all people labor on a 'hedonic treadmill.' As they rise in their accomplishments and possessions, their expectations also rise. Soon they habituate to the new level, and it no longer makes them happy. A similar phenomenon is found in the negative direction: interestingly, people are unhappy when they first encounter misfortune, but they soon adapt and it no longer makes them unhappy. On the basis of this reasoning, Brickman and Campbell proposed that people are destined to

---

[4]**Are the Rich Getting Richer and the Poor Getting Poorer?**
The Census Bureau has been studying the distribution of income since the late 1940's. The first income inequality statistics were published for families and came from the annual demographic supplement to the Current Population Survey (CPS). The most commonly used measure of income inequality, the Gini index (index of income concentration), indicated a decline in family income inequality of 7.4 percent from 1947 to 1968. Since 1968, there has been an increase in income inequality, reaching its 1947 level in 1982 and increasing further since then. The increase was 16.1 percent from 1968 to 1992 and 22.4 percent from 1968 to 1994. The Gini index ranges from 0.0, when every family (household) has the same income, to 1.0, when one family (household) has all the income. It is one way to measure how far a given income distribution is from equality. Living conditions of Americans have changed considerably since the late 1940's. In particular, a smaller fraction of all persons live in families (two or more persons living together related by blood or marriage). Therefore, starting in 1967, the Census Bureau began reporting on the

'hedonic neutrality' in the long run. For example, Silver (1982) found that persons with spinal cord injuries were extremely unhappy immediately after the accident that produced their disability, but quickly began to adapt. She found that within a matter of only eight weeks, positive emotions predominated over negative emotions. During this period, respondents experienced a downward trend in unpleasant emotions, and an upward trend in pleasant emotions, suggesting a return toward the baseline conditions of mood experienced by most people. This introduces the notion of a Set Point for happiness, similar to the Set-Point Theory of obesity[5]. But similar to new findings for obesity, the set-point for happiness can be raised or lowered depending on active work done by the individuals to raise or lower it.

> **And what is the point of leaving inherited wealth to your kids, as if that could bring *them* happiness?**

The Dangers of Materialism

"The greatest use of life is to spend it
for something that will outlast it."
William James

income distribution of households in addition to families. By coincidence, 1968 was the year in which measured postwar income was at its *most equal* for families. Since 1979, the Census Bureau has examined several experimental measures of income. These measures add the value of non-cash benefits (such as food stamps and employer contributions to health insurance) to, and subtract taxes from, the official money income measure. The Bureau's research in this area has shown that the distribution of income is more equal under a broadened definition of income that takes account of the effects of taxes and non-cash benefits. Further, government transfer benefits play a much more equalizing role on income than taxes. Nonetheless, while the levels of inequality are lower, this alternative perspective does not change the picture of increasing income inequality over the 1979 to 1994 period. The long-run increase in income inequality is related to changes in the Nation's labor market and its household composition. The wage distribution has become considerably more unequal with more highly skilled, trained, and educated workers at the top experiencing real wage gains and those at the bottom real wage losses.

We know it, sort of. Princeton sociologist Wuthnow (1998) reported that 89 percent of people report that "our society is much too materialistic." *Other* people in our society, that is, not *us*. Of this same group, 84 percent also wished they had more money, and 78 percent said it was "very or fairly important" to have a "beautiful home, a new car, and other nice things." But one wonders: what's the point? "Why," wondered the prophet Isiah, "do you spend your money for that which is not bread, and your labor for that which does not satisfy?" What's the point of accumulating stacks of unplayed CD's, closets full of seldom-worn designer clothes, garages with Bentley's–all purchased in pursuit of an elusive joy? And what is the point of leaving inherited wealth to your kids, as if *that* could bring them happiness?

The focus on the acquisition of material goods and direct pursuit of happiness is a far cry from the original view of even the materialists, such as John Locke, who were aware of the futility of pursuing happiness without qualifications, and who advocated the pursuit of happiness through "prudence"–making sure that people do not mistake imaginary happiness for real happiness.

---

[5]**The set point theory** holds that obesity entails a metabolic defect that functions as a homeostatic mechanism. This defect is supposed to result in a slowdown of resting metabolic rate in an overweight or obese individual who has lost weight. The resultant reduction in energy expenditure is said to be responsible for the often-observed scenario in which the individual regains the weight that was lost and thereby returns to his or her set point. However, support for the set point theory is limited to old data derived from outdated methods of physiologic measurement. Recent studies have challenged the theory (Rock (2003). These researchers have found that although a metabolic slowdown can occur during active weight loss, the slowdown ends once the patient reaches the target weight and shifts into weight-maintenance mode. Differences in physical activity are key in determining who will regain lost body weight.

Happiness Through 'Prudence'

What does it mean to pursue happiness through prudence? Epicurus, 2,300 years ago, said that to enjoy a happy life, one must develop *self-discipline*. The materialism of Epicurus was based on the ability to *defer gratification*. He claimed that although all pain was evil, this did not mean one should always avoid pain. For example, it made sense to put up with pain now, if one was sure to avoid a greater pain later. He wrote to his friend Menoeceus: "The beginning and the greatest good is prudence. For this reason, prudence is more valuable even than philosophy: from it derive all the other virtues. Prudence teaches us how impossible it is to live pleasantly without living wisely, virtuously, and justly . . . take thought, then, for these and kindred matters day and night . . . You shall be disturbed neither waking nor sleeping, and you shall live as a god among men. (Epicurus of Samos, trans. 1998, p. 48)

The popular view holds that we should grab pleasure and material comforts when we can, and that these alone will improve the quality of our lives. As technology has improved and lengthened our lives, we developed the hope that increased material rewards would bring about a better life. But research has shown again and again, that it is the ability to defer gratification that is not only the hallmark of a mature and responsible life, but the 'reversing consequence gradient' (see below) has been demonstrated as the key to a more deeply fulfilled life.

"The man of virtue makes the difficulty to be overcome his first business, and success only a subsequent consideration."
Confucius, The Confucian Analects

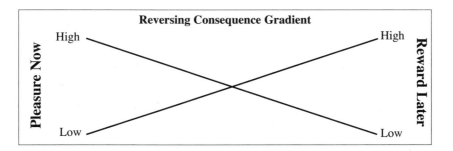

So, the popular view that we should grab pleasure and material comforts when we can, and that these alone will improve the quality of our live, didn't work out. People who live in the wealthiest industrialized Western nations are living in a period of unprecedented riches, in conditions that previous generations would have considered luxuriously comfortable, in relative peace and security, and they are living close to twice as long as their great grandparents did. Despite all these improvements in material conditions, people today are no more satisfied with their lives than their ancestors.

Material advantages do not translate into social and emotional benefits. To the extent that most of our energy becomes invested in material goals, sensitivity to other rewards atrophies. Friendship, art, literature, natural beauty, religion, and philosophy become less and less interesting, except as they pertain to acquisition. As early as 1970, Linder, the Swedish economist, pointed out that as income, and thus the value of one's time increases, it becomes less and less rational to spend it on anything besides making money, or on spending it conspicuously. The costs of playing with one's child, reading poetry, or attending a family reunion become too high, and so one stops doing such irrational things. Eventually, a person who only responds to material rewards becomes blind to any other kind and loses the ability to derive happiness from other sources (Benedikt, 1999). As is true of addiction in general, material rewards at first enrich the quality of life. Because of this, we tend to conclude that more must be better. But life is rarely linear; in most cases, what is good in small quantities becomes commonplace and then harmful in larger doses.

Eventually, a person who only responds to material rewards becomes blind to any other kind and loses the ability to derive happiness from other sources.

Our culture has eliminated alternatives that in previous times gave meaning and purpose to individual lives. Historians (e.g., Polanyi, 1957) claimed that past cultures provided a greater variety of attractive models for successful lives. A person could be valued and admired because he or she was a saint, a *bon vivant*, a wise person, a good craftsman, a brave patriot, or an upright citizen. These days, as we reduce everything to a quantifiable measure, the dollar is becoming the common metric by which to evaluate everything. Our worth is determined by the price we fetch in the marketplace. Unless a painting can get high bids at Sotheby's, it's not good art. A consultant is respected if he or she can charge five figures a day. It is not surprising that so many of us feel that our only hope for a happy life is to gather up all the earthly goods we can.

As the rich get richer, even those who are affluent are feeling poor. When we evaluate success, we use a strategy of escalating expectations, so that few people are ever satisfied for long with what they possess or what they have achieved. As more energy is invested in material goals, there is less left to pursue other goals that are also necessary for a life in which one aspires to happiness.

Material rewards do not detract from happiness. After a minimum threshold, which varies with the distribution of resources in the given society, they just become irrelevant.

Comparing Ourselves

Evolutionary psychologist Kenrick and his colleagues have shown that images of attractive models create psychological and social problems. In a series of studies on contrast effects, they discovered that men exposed to multiple images of attractive women, subsequently rated their commitment to their regular partner as lower, com-

> **These days, as we reduce everything to a quantifiable measure, the dollar is becoming the common metric by which to evaluate everything.**

pared with men exposed to average looking women (Kenrick, Neuberg, Zierk, & Krones, 1994). Women exposed to multiple images of dominant, high status men showed a similar decrease in commitment to, and love of, their regular partner, compared with women exposed repeatedly to less dominant men.

Repeated exposures affect self-concept as well. Women subjected to successive images of other women who are very attractive, subsequently feel less attractive themselves, showing a decrease in self-esteem (Gutierres, Kenrick, & Partch, 1999). Don't look at them! Men exposed to descriptions of highly dominant and influential men show a decrease in self-concept. Exposure to media images appears to lead to dissatisfactions with current partners and reductions in self-esteem and may interfere with the quality of close relationships, quality of life, and rates of depression.

Depression

Depression is, in fact, one of the most common psychological problems of modern humans, and afflicts twice as many women as men (Nolen-Hoeksema, 1987). Rates of depression are increasing in modern life. Five studies of 39,000 people living in five different parts of the world showed that young people are more likely than older people to have experienced at least one major episode of depression (Nesse & Williams, 1994, p. 220). One reason that depression is higher in more economically developed cultures (Nesse & Williams, 1994) is that mass communications, especially television and movies, make us all one competitive group even as they destroy our more intimate social networks.

In the ancestral environment, you would have had a good chance at being the best at something. Even if you were not the best, your group would likely value your skills. Now, we all compete with those who are the best in the world. Watching successful people on television arouses not inspiration, but envy. Although envy might have been useful to motivate our ancestors, now few of us can achieve the goals envy sets for us, and none of us can attain the fantasy lives we see on television (Nesse & Williams, 1994). Thus, the increase in depression develops in part, from self-perceived failures resulting in comparisons between our own lives, and the lives we see depicted so glamorously in the media.

Because of instant global communication, the standard is now set by the wealthiest nations. There is a common set of economic desires around the world, and national income is correlated with whether these desires can be met. People in China, India, and Nigeria now want cars, refrigerators, and DVDs; in other words, the world now wants what the West has, and their life satisfaction

60

reflects the progress they are making toward these goals. Unwittingly, we may be making the world unhappier and contributing to global unrest.

"To perceive is to suffer."
Aristotle

> **In the ancestral environment, you would have had a good chance at being the best at something.**

We know all this, and yet if we do not act, we do not know. More than 80 percent of the North American population regard the economic system as inherently unfair and the political system as a fraud, which serves the special interests, not the people.

Overwhelming majorities think:
a) Working people have too little voice in public affairs
b) The government has the responsibility of assisting people in need
c) Spending for education and health should take precedence over budget-cutting and tax cuts.

If we know it and don't do it,
we don't know it.

SUMMARY

That having more money to spend does not necessarily bring about greater subjective well being has also been documented on a national scale by Myers (1993). His calculations show that although the adjusted value of after-tax personal income in the United States has more than doubled between 1960 and 1990, the

> **More than 80 percent of the North American population regard the economic system as inherently unfair and the political system as a fraud, which serves the special interests, not the people.**

percentage of people describing themselves as "very happy" has remained unchanged at 30 percent (Myers, 1993, pp. 41-42).

1. You will not get happier with more money. If your basic needs are met, the road to happiness is the development of gratitude for what you have (see assessment in Appendix).

2. Happiness depends on your evaluations of events in your life, not on your possessions (but you knew that too). You won't get happier with age, but your expectations will be more realistic.

3. We were happier 40 years ago because we hoped for the future and we had fewer opportunities for social comparison.

ACTIONS

a) If you have responsibility for others in a leadership position, and you belive that happier people are healthier and more productive (they are), then plan your work activities so that goals are meaningful, quality of life and relationship-building are an important part of the work environment,

b) Because happiness can depend on the comparisons that we makewith 'how others are doing', make sure your social comparisons are sometimes slanted in your favor. If you have a habit of exposing yourself to idealized models, whether they be

Architectural Digest, Vogue or *US Magazine;* give yourself a break.

Do an experiment. Take a baseline 'contentment' rating using the 'Satisfaction with Life Scale' or the 'General Happiness Index' in the Appendix. For just one week, make a conscious effort to expose yourself to social comparisons that will lead to gratitude rather than envy. Visit poorer sections of your city, or travel to less fortunate countries. Volunteer to help others. Watch less television, and be conscious of the effect that commercials have on you. Then take the same assessment after your week and compare your scores. If they are even only *slightly* higher, wouldn't it be worthwhile to reconsider your social comparison models?

c) Don't buy into your kids' demands. Stop. You don't need them to like you, you need them to respect you. They will respect you if you do what is best for them–in the long run.

In Chapter Five, we'll examine how our world has improved, how we are making things better, and how we are making ourselves miserable in the process.

Chapter Five
If It Ain't Broke, Don't Break It. Well It's Broke.

Medical technology has reduced infant mortality in many parts of the world to a fraction of what it was in ancestral times. We have tools to prevent many diseases that afflicted our Stone Age forebears, and to alleviate symptoms of many others. Modern technology has given us the power to prevent pain associated with extremes of cold and heat, food shortages, some parasites, most predators, and other Darwinian (1859) "hostile forces of nature." In many ways, we live in comfort compared with our ancestors. We might not be happier, but we *are* getting better (Easterbrook, 2003).

But our modern environments have produced a variety of ills. Although we have the technology to combat food shortages, we now clog our arteries with animal fat and processed sugars (Nesse & Williams, 1994; Symons, 1987). We are producing skin cancers at alarming rates by depleting our ozone layer. Our ability to synthesize drugs has increased heroin addiction, cocaine abuse, and addiction to a variety of prescription drugs. In 2002, 69 percent of children (under 18 years) lived with two married parents, down from 77 percent in 1980). In 2001, 36 percent of U.S. households with children had one or more of the following three housing problems: physically inadequate housing, crowded housing or housing that cost more than 30 percent of the household income. (The rate rose from 30 percent in 1978 and has been stable since 1995.)

> **Although we have the technology to combat food shortages, we now clog our arteries with animal fat and processed sugars.**

Although happiness is difficult to measure directly (Kaheneman, 2001) one measure of our nation's 'happiness' might be the statistics on illegal drug use, poverty, violence, and other self-destructive behaviors such as smoking and alcoholism.

> *"Formerly, when religion was strong and science weak, men*
> *mistook magic for medicine; now, when science is strong and*
> *religion weak, men mistake medicine for magic."*
> *Thomas Szasz, Science and Scientism (1973)*

Zoloft, Prozac, and the Chemical High[6]

What of the current focus on Zoloft, Prozac and the chemical high? Every culture has developed drugs ranging from peyote to heroin to alcohol in an effort to improve mood or induce well being. Unfortunately, chemically induced well being lacks the core ingredient of happiness: the knowledge that one is responsible for having achieved it. Happiness is not something that happens to us, but something that we make happen. In some cultures,

---

[6]**Illicit drugs** include marijuana, cocaine (including crack), heroin, hallucinogens (including LSD, PCP, and ecstasy [MDMA]), amphetamines (including methamphetamine), and non-medical use of psychotherapeutics. Between 2001 and 2002, illicit drug use in the past 30 days declined from 23 percent to 21 percent among 10th-graders. One-quarter of 12th-graders and one-tenth of 8th-graders reported past-30-day illicit drug use in 2002, unchanged from the previous year. Drug use by adolescents can have immediate as well as long-term health and social consequences. Cocaine use is linked with health problems that range from eating disorders to disability to death from heart attacks and strokes (Blanken, 1993) Marijuana use poses both health and cognitive risks, particularly for damage to pulmonary functions as a result of chronic use (NIDA, 1995; Pope & Yurgelun-Todd, 1996). Hallucinogens can affect brain chemistry and result in problems with learning new information and memory (USPHS, 1993). Similar to alcohol use and smoking, drug use is a risk-taking behavior that has serious negative consequences.

Between 2001 and 2002, **illicit drug use** in the past 30 days declined from 23 percent to 21 percent among 10th-graders. One-quarter of 12th-graders and one-tenth of 8th-graders

drugs ingested in a ceremonial context appear to have lasting beneficial effects, but in such cases, the benefits result from performing the ritual, rather than from the chemicals. Humans need to use their own self-organizing abilities to achieve positive internal states through their own efforts, with minimal reliance on external manipulation of the nervous system. (There are times when these drugs are appropriate and recommenced. See criteria for depression and anxiety in the appendix.)

Youth, Substance Use, and the Media

"Children might or might not be a blessing, but to create
them and then fail them was surely damnation."
Lois McMaster Bujold, Barrayar, 1991

Over one-fifth (21%) of our 10th-graders and 29% of our 12th graders take illicit drugs. One in five 15-year-olds drinks heavily.[7] The role of substance use in prime time television is clear (Christensen, Henriksen and Roberts, 2000). Alcohol use was

---

reported past 30-day illicit drug use in 2002, unchanged from the previous year. Twelve-year trends for 8th- and 10th-graders show that past-30-day illicit drug use increased from the early to mid-1990s, peaking in 1996 at 15 percent and 23 percent in the respective grades. For 8th graders, illicit drug use declined gradually from 1996 to 2001 and decreased further in 2002; for 10th-graders, it remained stable until the decrease between 2001 and 2002. Longer-term trends for high school seniors show that past-30-day illicit drug use declined from 37 percent in 1980 to 14 percent in 1992. The rate then rose sharply, reaching 26 percent in 1997, and has remained around that level through 2002.

Among 12th-graders, more males than females report illicit drug use (29 percent compared with 22 percent, respectively, in 2002). For younger students, gender differences are less dramatic but are in the same direction. Between 2001 and 2002, past-30-day illicit drug use by males declined from 13 to 11 percent among 8th-graders and from 25 to 22 percent among 10th-graders; illicit drug use by females in these grades remained stable over this period.

portrayed in 77 percent of all episodes surveyed. Over 40 percent of the episodes made drinking alcohol look like a positive experience, and only 10 percent of the episodes was there portrayed the use of alcohol as a negative experience. Nearly half the episodes (45 percent) associated alcohol use with humor. As noted in our footnote, below, alcohol use has declined, but a decline is no victory; for any of our children to report episodic heavy drinking is alarming. Alcohol is the most commonly used psychoactive substance during adolescence, and its use is associated with motor vehicle accidents, injuries, and deaths; with problems in school and in the workplace; and with fighting, crime, and other serious consequences. Early onset of heavy drinking is especially problematic, potentially increasing the likelihood of mental and physical illness as well as emotional and societal problems. The level of youth violence in society can be viewed as an indicator of our youths' ability to control their behavior, as well as the adequacy of socializing agents such as families, peers, schools, and religious institutions to supervise or channel youth behavior to acceptable norms.

---

[7]**Alcohol Use**
One in five 15-year-olds drink heavily. From 2001 to 2002, the proportion of 10th-graders reporting episodic heavy drinking (i.e., having at least five drinks in a row at least once in the previous 2 weeks) declined from 25 percent to 22 percent. Rates remained stable from 2001 to 2002 among 8th- and 12th-graders, with 12 and 29 percent, respectively, reporting this type of alcohol consumption in 2002. Long-term trends for high school seniors indicate a peak in 1981, when 41 percent reported heavy drinking. Over the next 12 years, the percentage of high school seniors reporting heavy drinking declined gradually to a low of 28 percent in 1993. Since 1993, this prevalence has not decreased. Not surprisingly, among 12th-graders, males are more likely to drink heavily than are females. In 2002, 34 percent of 12th-grade males reported heavy drinking, compared with 23 percent of 12th-grade females. As adolescents get older, the differences between males and females in this drinking behavior appear to become more pronounced. Among 10th-graders, the gender difference in heavy drinking has been found in earlier years (e.g., 29 percent for males versus 21 percent for females in 2001), but a sharp decline in drinking among males brought the rates closer in 2002 (24 percent for males versus 21 percent for females).

Violence

Violence[8] affects the quality of life of young people who experience, witness, or feel threatened by it. In addition to the direct physical harm suffered by young victims of serious violence, such violence can adversely affect victims' mental health and development and increase the likelihood that they themselves will commit acts of serious violence. Youth, ages 12 to 17, are twice as likely as adults to be *victims* of serious violent crimes, which include aggravated assault, rape, robbery (stealing by force or threat of violence), and homicide.

"Teen-agers account for the largest portion of all violent crime in America. They're the predators out there. They're the most violent criminals on the face of the earth." U.S. Representative Bill McCollum (R-FL), 1996 "...while juveniles accounted for about 19 percent of all violent crime arrests in 1994 (down from 23 percent in 1973), respondents to national polls believe that juveniles commit 43 percent of all violent crime." *Christian Science Monitor,* Nov 1997.

---

[8]**Violence**

One alarming measure is the incidence rate of serious violent juvenile crime. According to reports by victims, in 2000 the serious violent crime offending rate was 17 crimes per 1,000 juveniles ages 12 to 17, totaling 413,000 such crimes involving juveniles. This is a 67 percent drop from the 1993 high and the lowest rate recorded since the national victimization survey began in 1973. Reports by victims indicate that between 1980 and 1989, the serious violent juvenile crime offending rate fluctuated between 29 and 40 per 1,000, and then began to increase from 34 per 1,000 in 1989 to a high of 52 per 1,000 in 1993. Since then, the rate has steadily dropped, to 17 per 1,000 in 2000.

Based on victims' reports, since 1980 the percentage of all serious violent crime involving juveniles has ranged from 19 percent in 1982 to 26 percent in 1993, the peak year for youth violence. In 2000, 19 percent of all such victimizations reportedly involved a juvenile offender. In more than half (59 percent) of all serious violent juvenile crimes reported by victims in 2000, more than one offender was involved in the incident. Because insufficient detail exists to determine the age of each individual offender when a crime is committed

The mixed messages from the popular media are confusing. The American rags-to-riches Horatio Alger stories are unrealistic parables suggesting that anything and everything is possible. These are seen side-by-side on the evening news with horror stories about the present state of the world. We are driving our kids nuts.

> **The mixed messages from the popular media are confusing. We are driving our kids nuts.**

In addition, there is a disturbingly large amount of violence available through the media, and particularly on televised children's programs. But not all violence is the same. Researchers from four universities announced findings of what they described as the most comprehensive scientific assessment of television violence ever conducted. Funded by the National Cable Television Association, the study reported that industry-wide, 57 percent of the programs surveyed showed some kind of violence with premium cable channels containing the most violence. There was violence in 85 percent of their programming. On network television, 44 percent of programming included violence. And on public television, 18 percent of programs showed violence.

More important than the portrayal of violence was its resolution. In 47 percent of all violent acts no harm was shown to victims, and in 73 percent of the violent scenes, the perpetrators were

---

by more than one offender, the number of additional juvenile offenders cannot be determined. Therefore, this rate of serious violent crime offending does not represent the number of juvenile offenders in the population, but rather the number of crimes committed involving juveniles ages 12 to 17 in relation to the juvenile population. NOTE: Serious violent crimes include aggravated assault, rape, robbery (stealing by force or threat of violence), and homicide.

unpunished. About three-quarters of all programs have scenes of violence in which there is no punishment. That means the hero is rewarded in some way, or the criminal gets away with it, or something similar.

Negative Effects of Viewing Violence

There are three primary types of antisocial effects of concern that are associated with a heavy dose of violent viewing.

> **Children's programming is among the worst; because it often depicts violence in a humorous context, which trivializes it and makes it feel acceptable.**

1) Learning aggressive attitudes and behaviors.
2) Desensitization to the victims or the harms that are suffered by victims of violence.
3) Fear of being victimized by violence.

Children's programming poses two particular issues:

1. When violence is shown, it rarely describes or includes any depictions of long-term negative consequences. For example, if you commit violence, are you ashamed? Are you socially stigmatized, or is it demonstrated clearly that this is unacceptable behavior that has tremendous costs? Also, violence really hurts. It's not clean and sanitized, as you might see on television.

2. Children's programming is among the worst; because it often depicts violence in a humorous context, which trivializes it and makes it feel acceptable.

71

Poverty[9]

*"Poverty is the parent of
revolution and crime."*
Aristotle

According to the Census Bureau, the proportion of Americans living in poverty rose significantly in 2002, increasing for the first
time in eight years. In addition, the bureau reported that the
income of middle-class households fell for the first time since the
last recession ended, in 1991. The Census Bureau's annual report
on income and poverty provided stark evidence that the weaken-
ing economy had begun to affect large segments of the population, regardless of race, region or class. Daniel H. Weinberg, chief
of income and poverty statistics at the Census Bureau, said the
recession that began in March 2001 had reduced the earnings of

---

[9]**Poverty**

Wade F. Horn, the U.S. welfare director, said the number of poor children was "much
lower than in 1996," when Congress overhauled the welfare law to impose strict work
requirements. Of the 32.9 million poor people in the United States last year, 11.7 million
were under 18, and 3.4 million were 65 or older. Poverty rates for children, 16.3 percent,
and the elderly, 10.1 percent, were unchanged from 2000. But the poverty rate for people
18 to 64 rose to 10.1 (Janet, you circled this, but I don't' know why) percent. Median
household income for blacks fell in 2002 by $1,025, or 3.4 percent, to $29,470. Median
income of Hispanics, at $33,565, was unchanged. But household income fell by 1.3 per-
cent for non-Hispanic whites, to $46,305, and by 6.4 percent for Asian Americans, to
$53,635. There were 6.8 million poor families in 2002, up from 6.4 million in 2000. The
poverty rate for families rose to 9.2 percent, from a 26-year low of 8.7 percent in 2000.
The rate in the South rose to 13.5 percent, from 12.8 percent in 2000. The South is home
to more than 40 percent of all the nation's poor, and it accounted for more than half of the
national increase in the number of poor last year. The poverty rate for the suburbs rose to
8.2 percent last year, from 7.8 percent in 2000. The number of poor people in suburban
areas rose by 700,000, to 12 million. There was virtually no change in the rates in central
cities (16.5 percent) and outside metropolitan areas (14.2 percent).The bureau said the
number of "severely poor" rose to 13.4 million last year, from 12.6 million in 2000. People
are considered to be severely poor if their family incomes are less than half of the official
poverty level.

millions of Americans. The report also suggested that the gap between rich and poor continues to grow.

The Census Bureau said the number of poor Americans rose, in 2002, to 32.9 million, an increase of 1.3 million, while the proportion living in poverty rose to 11.7 percent, from 11.3 percent in 2000. Median household income fell to $42,228 in 2001,

> **The gap between rich and poor continues to grow. The middle-class is being squeezed out.**

a decline of $934 or 2.2 percent from the prior year. The number of households with income above the median is the same as the number below it. A family of four was classified as poor if it had cash income less than $18,104 last year. The official poverty level, updated each year to reflect changes in the Consumer Price Index, was $14,128 for a family of three, $11,569 for a married couple and $9,039 for an individual. 'Severely poor' is defined as half that amount. Could you live on $375 a month? Over 13.4 million of us do.

President Bush however, remained "optimistic" (*New York Times*, September 25, 2003). "When you combine the productivity of the American people with low interest rates and low inflation, those are the ingredients for growth."

Smoking
"To see what is right, and not to do it, is
want of courage or of principle."
Confucius

The good news is that rates are decreasing; the bad news is that any of our nation's children still smoke. In 2002, daily cigarette use among 8th-, 10th-, and 12th-graders reached its lowest point since the beginning of the Monitoring the Future Survey (5 percent, 10 percent, and 17 percent, respectively), continuing the downward trend that began in 1997 for 12th-graders and in 1996 for 10th- and 8th-graders.

In the Wakefield, Flay, Nichter, Giovino (2002) comprehensive review, the authors concluded that:

a) the media both shapes and reflects social values about smoking;

b) the media provides new information about smoking directly to audiences;

c) the media acts as a source of observational learning by providing models which teenagers may seek to emulate;

d) exposure to media messages about smoking also provides direct reinforcement for smoking or not smoking.

Media messages are endemic in our society, through exposure to television and radio, movies, outdoor and point of sale advertising, via newspapers and magazines, on the internet and through books, brochures and posters. In the United States, more families own a television than a telephone (Nielsen Media Research, 1995). Given a conservative estimate of 2.5 hours of watching TV each day over a lifetime, and assuming eight hours of sleep per night, the average American would spend seven years out of the approximately 47 waking years we have by age 70 watching TV (Kubey & Csikszentmihalyi, 1998).

Young people average 16 to 18 hours of television watching per week, commencing at age *two* (American Medical Association, 1996). These reports have noted that it is not uncommon to find infants under the age of six months propped in front of the television-as-babysitter. Over half of all 15 to 16 year-olds have seen the majority of the most popular recent R-rated movies (Greenberg et al., 1987) and almost all have seen a copy of *Playboy* or *Playgirl* by the age of 15 (Brown & Bryant, 1989). In addition, the internet continues to increase in accessibility and popularity, exposing users to a wide range of information, previously not so accessible.

> **Young people average 16 to 18 hours of television watching per week, starting at age two. The average American spends seven years of his life watching TV.**

Many of the media messages about smoking come in the form of paid advertising from tobacco companies, through promotions which offer accessories and clothing with cigarette brands emblazoned on them, and other communications about smoking which appear in the context of movies, in television programs and through sponsorships. Making matters worse, celebrities such as Whoopi Goldberg, smoking during her 2003-4 TV series, seemed unconcerned with her impact on youth.

Obesity

The "Concert For World Children's Day" Theme Song "Aren't They All Our Children," won a 2003 Emmy Award. The song was written as part of World Children's Day at McDonald's™, an international fund-raising effort benefiting Ronald McDonald House Charities, and performed at Ronald McDonald House

Charities' 18th Annual Awards of Excellence, in which outstanding individuals who have made significant contributions to improve the lives of children, are recognized. Isn't that Great?

The event's press release stated that to date, Ronald McDonald House Charities' national body and global network of local Chapters have awarded more than $380 million to children's programs. However, nowhere in the press release did it mention that obesity is costing our nation over $270 million dollars *each* day (Geary, 2002), or that fast food is a significant part of that problem.

> **However, nowhere in the press release did it mention that obesity is costing our nation over $270 million dollars *each* day.**

The proportion of children ages 6 to 18 who are overweight more than doubled over the past two decades. It shot up from 6 percent in 1976-1980 to 15 percent in 1999-2000. Racial, ethnic, and gender disparities exist, such that in 1999-2000, Black, non-Hispanic girls and Mexican American boys were at particularly high risk of being overweight (24 percent and 29 percent, respectively). Overweight adolescents often become overweight adults, with an increased risk for a wide variety of poor health outcomes including diabetes, stroke, heart disease, arthritis and certain cancers.

The immediate consequences of overweight in childhood are often psycho-social, but also include cardiovascular risk factors such as high blood pressure, high cholesterol, and the precursors to diabetes (Dietz, 1998). The prevalence of excess weight among children changed relatively little from the early 1960's through 1980; however, since 1980 it has increased sharply in both the

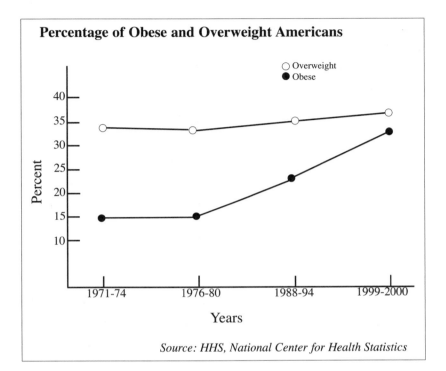

Percentage of Obese and Overweight Americans

○ Overweight
● Obese

Source: HHS, National Center for Health Statistics

U.S. and Europe (Ogden et al., 2002) and is finally the subject of popular and alarming reports ('Cut the Fat,' *Consumer Reports,* January 2004, pp. 12-16).

To let us all off the hook, reports state that "the reasons for the increase in children who are overweight are not clear. Numerous factors such as advances in technology and trends in eating out have been suggested as causes; however, definitive data linking these factors to the recent trends are lacking." They do state that "on an individual basis, it is clear that overweight results from an imbalance between energy intake and energy expenditure."

According to the National Center for Chronic Disease Prevention

For more information about the role of the media and the fast-food industry in our nation's obesity problem, see:

Eric Schlosser: *Fast Food Nation*

Barbara Ehrenreich: *Nickel and Dimed: On (Not) Getting By in America*

Michael Moore: *Stupid White Men ...and Other Sorry Excuses for the State of the Nation*

Marion Nestle: *Food Politics: How the Food Industry Influences Nutrition and Health*

John De Graaf, et al: *Affluenza: The All-Consuming Epidemic*

Greg Critser: *Fat Land : How Americans Became the Fattest People in the World*

and Health Promotion, only half of American children participate in vigorous physical activity, and less than a quarter eat the recommended five or more servings of fruits and vegetables per day (Grunbaum et al., 2002), both of which are likely to contribute to the current high rates of overweight.

These reports do not mention the domination of the media over our children's lives, including entry into their classrooms and textbooks with their advertisers dictating clothing style, food choice, and entertainment. These reports do not mention that Burger King Double Whopper with Cheese has 960 calories with 63grams of fat (GF), BK Big Fish has 700 calories and 44 GF, MacDonald's Hotcakes contain 580 calories and 16 GF, an Arch Deluxe w/Bacon 590 calories and 34 grams GF. Add a large Coca-Cola at 310 calories or an innocent-sounding Chocolate Shake Small for 360 calories and you have the daily caloric allotment for sedentary children. *(Source: Fast Food*

Nutrition fact Finder http://www.fatcalories.com/ and Fast Food Facts by the Minnesota Attorney General's Office).

Some authors have begun to walk the long road toward truth. Schlosser's (2001) history of the development of American fast food indicted the industry for crimes against humanity, including systematically destroying the American diet and landscape, and undermining our values and our economy. He points out that each day, one out of four of us eat food from a fast-food restaurant. A 15-year Harvard Medical School study of 3,700 young adults found that eating fast food more than twice a week increased the risk of obesity more than 50 percent (*Consumer Reports*, January 2004, p. 13)

Fast food is so ubiquitous that it is now seen around the world as American, and as harmless, as apple pie. But the industry's drive for homogenization and speed has transformed America's diet, landscape, economy, and workforce in insidiously destructive ways, from the overworked and underpaid teenage workers, to the factory farms to the slaughterhouses.

SUMMARY

a)   Medical technology has reduced infant mortality in many parts of the world to a fraction of what it was in ancestral times. We have tools to prevent many diseases that afflicted our fore-bears, and to alleviate symptoms of many others. In many ways, we are getting better.

b)   Self-destructive behaviors such as smoking, illicit drug use, and overeating have increased dramatically.

c)   Poverty is increasing, especially among the middle and lower-classes. Mass material consumption has played a large role.

d) The media has played a significant role in all these problems.

ACTION

1. Choose your television viewing carefully, and limit or curtail viewing by children. Do not permit viewing of violent programs. Your children will tell you that all the kids watch those programs; ignore them.

2. Cut down on buying items that depreciate with age. Not only is it the quickest path to poverty, it encourages the Positive Spin system. If it will *make* you money (appreciate with time), get it. If it will cost you money, don't get it. Nobody cares how much you have. Honestly, it doesn't matter.

3. Write and call your elected officials complaining about what we've discussed in this chapter. They do listen to what will get them re-elected. If enough of us write or call, we *can* change the system.

4. My comments on smoking and fast food are meant to be self-explanatory. Don't smoke and avoid fast food. YES YOU CAN.

Next, we'll test out the getting-happy-by-moving-around, or the grass-is-greener, theory.

Chapter Six
"Maybe We Should Move to California"

"Wherever you go, there you are."
Old Saying

Individualistic cultures, such as the American culture, stress the importance of the individual and his or her thoughts, choices, and feelings. Collectivist cultures such as Japan, China, and to some extent Canada and Sweden, require that people sacrifice their desires to the will of the group. When deciding how satisfied they are, people in individualistic nations consult their emotions; if they feel pleasant emotions they feel satisfied. Those from collectivist cultures consult norms for whether they should be satisfied, and to check in with family and friends. Thus, people differ across societies in the factors they consider to be relevant to life satisfaction.

> **When deciding how satisfied they are, Americans consult their emotions; if they feel pleasant emotions, they feel satisfied. Thus, you won't be more satisfied anywhere else unless you first change your emotional state.**

Individualistic nations report higher life satisfaction, and yet suicide rates are also higher (Diener, 1996). There are high rates of marital satisfaction in individualistic nations, but the divorce rates are also high. People in individualistic societies say they are happy with their circumstances, yet they more often change them. When people in societies with more freedom are satisfied with their marriages or jobs, they stay with them, but individualists are more likely to change their circumstances when they are dissatisfied.

81

Inglehart (1990) proposed that as basic material needs are met, individuals move to a post-materialistic phase in which they are concerned with self-fulfillment. So should you move to an individualist or collectivist culture to be happier? Well, read the above, and think about it carefully.

> **The U.S. population rated money more important than either life satisfaction or happiness, and claimed that they thought about it more often as well.**

An international college sample of 7,204 respondents in 42 diverse countries shows how students view happiness (Suh, Diener, Oishi, & Triandis, 1998). Mean values are shown below for how how important happiness was to them. Even in non-western societies, students reported that happiness and life satisfaction were very important, and said they thought about them often. Although respondents in the most westernized nations granted happiness greater importance, mean levels of concern about happiness were high in all countries surveyed. Among the total sample, only six percent of respondents rated money as more important than happiness. But, guess what? The U.S. population rated money more important than either life satisfaction or happiness, and claimed that they thought about it more often as well.

The World Values Survey (World Values Study Group, 1994), using representative samples of 1,000 respondents per nation found, between 1990 and 1993, that the correlation between purchasing power, income, and average life satisfaction was .62 across all nations in the survey. Wealthier nations do have higher levels of reported well being because they are more likely to fulfill basic human needs for food, shelter, and health, as well as to have better human-rights records (Diener et al., 1995). However,

Importance of Subjective Well Being to College Students

How important is:

Nation	Life satisfaction	Happiness	Money
Argentina	6.67	6.78	4.46
Australia	6.59	6.66	4.44
Bahrain	6.08	6.21	5.01
China	5.67	5.91	4.82
Germany	6.62	5.95	4.11
Greece	6.73	6.77	4.89
Hungary	6.43	6.57	4.30
India	5.75	5.97	4.81
Indonesia	6.16	6.63	4.89
Japan	6.02	6.31	4.70
Lithuania	6.18	6.62	5.23
Singapore	6.25	6.59	4.80
Slovenia	6.78	6.62	4.60
South Africa	6.44	6.61	5.00
Tanzania	5.06	5.45	5.17
Turkey	6.25	5.75	5.25
US	**6.39**	**6.58**	**6.68**

Note: The 1 to 7 "How often do you think about?" scale was anchored by 1 (never), 4 (sometimes), and 7 (very much, several times a day or more). Importance ratings were reported on a 1-7 scale, where 1 was of no importance whatsoever and 7 was extraordinarily important and valuable.*(Suh, Diener, Oishi, & Triandis, 1998)*

there were countries that were unexpectedly high or low in life satisfaction even after income was controlled. Mean levels of happiness in Brazil, Chile, and Argentina were higher than predicted by their wealth. Life-satisfaction rates in Eastern European nations and Russia were low, even after controlling for income. The higher-than-expected scores in Latin American nations may have been due to cultural factors, (hey, maybe great wines and beef *can* cheer you up) whereas the lower-than-expected scores in former communist countries may have been due to the political and economic turmoil in these nations during the years of the survey. Japan appeared as an outlier, with high income and relatively low happiness, but Japan as a highly regulated society with strong conformity pressures and very high expectations was expected to yield these scores.

The most surprising finding, and the one most salient to our purposes, was that happiness has not increased regularly over the years in the nations where repeated surveys have been conducted,[10] despite dramatic income increases (Diener & Oishi, 2001; Myers, 2000). So the question became: "Why don't increases in income in the wealthiest nations produce increases in happiness?"

> **Increases in income in the wealthiest nations do not raise levels of happiness because people's desires are driven by the rising living standard.**

Increases in income in the wealthiest nations do not raise levels of happiness because people's desires are driven by the rising living standard. As income rises, so does the evaluative standard. The rich get richer but they don't get happier. Increases in income in the wealthiest nations have not increased happiness. Feelings of wealth depend more on the level of your desires than on your income. Lasting happiness comes from working for one's goals (Emmons, 1986), close social relationships (Myers, 2000), and being involved in 'flow' activities (Csikszentmihalyi, 1997), not acquisition. We will explore these concepts in depth in Chapters 11-13.

---

[10]*Source: World Bank. 2003. World Development Indicators 2003. CD-ROM. Washington, DC.* It is beyond the scope of this book to present complete data; for a complete report see Human Development Report 2003 Millennium Development Goals: A compact among nations to end human poverty at http://www.undp.org/hdr2003/

National statistics of social pathology show that people in the western world today are not happier than their ancestors were. As we noted in Chapter Five, violent crimes have tripled, family breakdown doubled, and psychosomatic complaints have increased exponentially since the 1950's. If material well being leads to happiness, why is capitalist affluence becoming increasingly addicted to drugs for falling asleep, waking up, staying slim, escaping boredom and dealing with depression? Why are suicides and loneliness such a problem in Sweden, which has applied the best of socialist principles to provide material security to its people?

Although cross-national comparisons show a correlation between the wealth of a country, as measured by its gross national product, and the self-reported happiness of its inhabitants (Inglehart, 1990), we find the people of Germany and Japan, with more than twice the gross national product of Ireland, report much lower levels of happiness. In a study of the relationship between material and subjective well being in some of the wealthiest individuals in the United States, Diener, Horwitz, and Emmons (1985), found their levels of happiness to be barely above that of individuals with average incomes.

> **In affluent countries, where most can afford life's necessities, affluence matters little.**

The Swiss and Scandinavians are prosperous and satisfied. When people in poorer nations compare their lifestyles with the abundance of those in rich nations, they may become more aware of their relative poverty. However, among nations with a gross national product of more than $8,000 per person, the correlation between national wealth and well being evaporates. During the 1980's, the Irish reported consistently greater life satisfaction than did the much wealthier but less satisfied West Germans (Inglehart, 1990). National wealth is entangled with civil rights, literacy, and the number of continuous years of democracy.[11]

In poor countries such as India, where low income threatens basic human needs, more often, being relatively well off predicts greater well being (Argyle, 1999). It is better to be high caste than low. In affluent countries, where most can afford life's necessities, affluence matters little. In the United States, Canada, and Europe, the correlation between income and personal happiness is negligible. Happiness tends to be lower among the very poor. Once comfortable, however, more money provides diminishing returns on happiness. Lykken (1999) observed that "People who go to work in their overalls and on the bus are just as happy, on the average, as those in suits who drive to work in their own Mercedes" (p. 17).

Economist Robert Frank (1996) has described his experience with this phenomenon:

> "As a young man fresh out of college, I served as
> a Peace Corps Volunteer in rural Nepal. My one-
> room house had no electricity, no heat, no indoor
> toilet, no running water. The local diet offered lit-

---

[11]**The Gini index** measures the extent to which the distribution of income (or consumption) among individuals or households within a country deviates from a perfectly equal distribution. A Lorenz curve plots the cumulative percentages of total income received against the cumulative number of recipients, starting with the poorest individual or household. The Gini index measures the area between the Lorenz curve and a hypothetical line of absolute equality, expressed as a percentage of the maximum area under the line. A value of 0 represents perfect equality, a value of 100 perfect inequality.

tle variety and virtually no meat. . . Yet, although my living conditions in Nepal were a bit startling at first, the most salient feature of my experience was how quickly they came to seem normal. Within a matter of weeks, I lost all sense of impoverishment. Indeed, my $40 monthly stipend was more than most others had in my village, and with it I experienced a feeling of prosperity that I have recaptured only in recent years."

The range of human development in the world is vast and uneven, with astounding progress in some areas amidst stagnation and dismal decline in others. There is a clear and positive relationship between equality of income and quality of life in all nations. This translates directly to happiness levels, because of the differing values placed on happiness and the differing definitions.

Jealousy, Or Comparing Ourselves to Others

"Nature does nothing uselessly."
Aristotle, Politics

Jealousy is an evolved psychological mechanism designed to combat the adaptive problem of threat to valued long-term mateships (Daly et al., 1982; Symons, 1979). Jealousy functions to alert a person to a mate's possible or actual infidelity and motivates action designed to prevent infidelity or deal with defection. Jealousy is a distressing emotion, a passion dangerous to the self and to others (Buss, 2000). It can cause sleepless nights, cause a person to question his or her worth as a mate, create anxiety about losing a partner, and play havoc with social reputation. **Jealousy used to provide an adaptive function in our evolutionary past,** in that those who were indifferent to the sexual contact of their mates lost the evolutionary contest. The legacy of this success is a dangerous passion that creates unhappiness, but the unhappiness motivated adaptive action over human evolutionary history (Buss, 2000). Modern jealousy is tethered to events that would have caused fitness failure in ancestral times. Jealousy has emerged in unprecedented ways in the modern corporation. If leadership does not ensure that workers develop a vision of a larger social context, in which one's connection to the whole is understood and keenly felt, then jealousy can wreak havoc on the team's productivity.

> **If leadership does not ensure that workers develop a vision of a larger social context, in which one's connection to the whole is understood and keenly felt, then jealousy can wreak havoc on the team's productivity.**

Jealousy is no longer an adaptive mechanism, and our unwillingness to release it is causing us misery, and the costing the corporate world in lost production and wasted energies.

People experience jealousy when:
Someone blocks their ascension in the social hierarchy
They suffer a slide in status
A friend betrays them
Their coalition is weakened
Their team loses
Their health is impaired
A sibling is favored over them by a parent
They are victimized by malicious gossip
A partner rejects them for another mate

Natural selection operates on differences, so one person's gain is often another person's loss. As Symons (1979) observed, "the most fundamental, most universal double standard is not male versus female but each individual human versus everyone else" (p. 229). The implication of this is that humans have evolved psychological mechanisms designed to inflict costs on others, to gain advantage at the expense of others, to delight in the downfall of others, and to envy those who are more successful at achieving the goals toward which they aspire. Do people feel especially good about themselves when superseding or subordinating others (Gilbert, 1989)? Are envy and depression reliable consequences of being relatively low in the social hierarchy (Gilbert, 1989; Price & Slornan, 1987)? Given the apparent universality of status hierarchies in all groups and all cultures worldwide, escape from relative ranking is difficult. We need to update our thinking.

Modern living creates a paradox (Tooby & Cosmides, 1996). Humans act to avoid personal trouble, and in modern living, many of the hostile forces of nature that would have killed us have now been controlled. Many people who are alive today would have been devoured by lions a few hundred years ago, for example, the idiot ahead of you on the highway. Laws deter stealing, assault, and murder. A police force performs many of the functions previously performed by friends. Medical science has eliminated or reduced many sources of disease and illness. People live in an environment that in many ways is safer and more stable than the environment inhabited by their ancestors.

SUMMARY

When deciding how satisfied they are, Americans consult their emotions; if they feel pleasant emotions, they feel satisfied. Thus, you won't be more satisfied anywhere else unless you first change your emotional state.

However, be aware that Americans think about money more than any other nation; thus, as you absorb the culture of your new nation, you might report higher satisfaction levels.

In the following chapter, we explore the truth of how some of our systems have contributed to this perfect storm of unhappiness.

Chapter Seven
Snow White Was A Snow Job

"The stupid neither forgive nor forget;
the naive forgive and forget; the wise forgive but do not forget."
Thomas Szasz, The Second Sin, Personal Conduct, (1973)

Societies are structured so that the great majority must believe that their well being depends on being passive and contented consumers. Whether the leadership is in the hands of a priesthood, merchants, or financiers, their interest is to have the rest of the population depend on whatever rewards they have to offer–be it eternal life, security, or material comfort. If you buy the right car, the right vodka, or the right watch, we will guarantee your happiness, even if doing so will mortgage your life.

Materialist propaganda is clever and convincing. It is not so easy, especially for young people, to tell what is truly in their interest from what will only harm them in the long run. This is why John Locke, as we saw in Chapter Three, cautioned people not to mistake imaginary happiness for real happiness. It is also why, 25 centuries ago, Plato wrote that the most urgent task for educators is to teach young people to find pleasure in the right things.

"Pleasure in the job puts
perfection in the work." Aristotle

"I've grown to realize the joy that comes from little
victories is preferable to the fun that comes from ease
and the pursuit of pleasure."
Lawana Blackwell,
The Courtship of the Vicar's Daughter, 1998

91

Our Healers' Role in the Perfect Storm

Psychiatrists and psychologists understand how people survive under conditions of adversity, but know little about how healthy people flourish under neutral conditions. Psychiatry, in its concentration on repairing damage within a disease model, has neglected the fulfilled individual and the thriving community. The exclusive focus on pathology has resulted in a model of the human being lacking the positive features that make life worth living. Hope, wisdom, creativity, future mindedness, courage, spirituality, responsibility, and perseverance are explained as transformations of more authentic negative impulses.

A search of *Psychological Abstracts* since 1887 revealed 8,072 articles on anger, 57,800 on anxiety, and 70,856 on depression. Only 851 abstracts mentioned joy, 2,958 happiness, and 5,701 life satisfaction. In this sampling, negative emotions topped positive emotions by a 14-to-1 ratio.

If the old saying is true that "whatever we pay attention
to gets stronger," then by focusing relentlessly on what's wrong,
we have been increasing rates of disorder.
New drugs find new diagnoses to fill.

Why has psychology and much of western academic world adopted the premise that negative motivations are the authentic ones, and positive emotions are derivative? It could be that negative emotions and experiences are more urgent, and thus override positive ones. Negative emotions reflect immediate problems or objective dangers, so are powerful enough to force people to stop, increase vigilance, reflect on, and change their actions. Thus, negative emotions are seen as powerful, action-oriented and male. When we are adapting, no such alarm is needed. Experiences that create or promote true happiness often seem to develop effortlessly.

The masculine bias in psychology, together with the focus on the negative may reflect differences in the survival value of negative versus positive emotions. Perhaps, however, people are unaware of the survival value of posi-

> **The masculine bias in psychology, together with the focus on the negative may reflect differences in the survival value of negative versus positive emotions.**

tive emotions, precisely because they are so important. Like the fish who is unaware of the water in which it swims, people take for granted a certain amount of hope, love, enjoyment, and trust because these are the very conditions that allow them to go on living. These conditions are fundamental to existence, and if they are present, any number of objective obstacles can be faced with equanimity and even joy. One cannot answer that question just by curing depression; there must be positive reasons for living as well.

In the 50-75 years since psychology and psychiatry became healing disciplines, they have developed a usable taxonomy, reliable ways of measuring such concepts as schizophrenia, anger, and depression, and developed sophisticated methods for understanding causal pathways that lead to such undesirable outcomes. Most important, they developed pharmacological and psychological interventions that have allowed many untreatable disorders to become treatable. Thus, the whole industry has been hugely invested in the diagnosis-treatment business.

Despite recent protests spearheaded by Seligman (1998, 2002) that psychology should focus as much on strength as on weakness, be interested as much in resilience as in vulnerability, and as occupied with wellness as with pathology, not much has changed. A doctoral dissertation doesn't sound as punchy–as academic–with those pesky positive terms in them. Despite over 1,780 self-help books emphasizing positive thinking (Amazon.com, January 2004), we still aren't happy. It could be that our definition of happiness is askew; that we are chasing a golden ring that is ever removed further and further from us.

> **Freud felt that we could best discover human nature by examining where it was cracked. This disease focus became prevalent in our Western world.**

Optimism, and being 'positive,' have received bad press not only from psychology, however. Voltaire's (1759) Dr. Pangloss was portrayed as a naïve idiot when he declared that we "live in the best of all possible worlds," and Porter's (1913) Pollyanna celebrated every misfortune befalling herself and others. Politicians compete to see who can best spin negative news stories into something useful; even positive spins have gotten negative reviews.

Admittedly, early approaches to optimism as human nature were negative. Sophocles 496-406 BC (Winnington-Ingram, 2002) and Nietzsche (Gay & Kaufmann, 2000) argued that optimism prolongs human suffering: it is better to face the hard facts of reality. This view formed the basis of Freud's teachings. In *The Future of an Illusion*, Freud (1928) decided that optimism was widespread, but illusory. According to Freud, optimism helps make civiliza-

Life As Tragedy

A long tradition views life as tragedy. From Sophocles' in Oedipus at Colonus that "Not to be born is, past all prizing, best" to Woody Allen's observations of "two kinds of lives: the horrible and the merely miserable" (Annie Hall, 1977).

Jean-Jacques Rousseau (1712-1778): "Our pains greatly exceed our pleasures, so that, all things considered, human life is not at all a valuable gift."

Samuel Johnson (1709-1784): "We are not born for happiness."

Sigmund Freud (1928): "One feels inclined to say that the intention that man should be happy is not included in the plan of Creation."

Albert Camus (1913-1960): "The foremost question of philosophy is why one should not commit suicide."

Bertrand Russell (1872-1970) in *The Conquest of Happiness*: "Most people are unhappy."

Anatole France (1844-1924): "The average man does not know what to do with his life, yet wants another one which will last forever. . . .For France, the essence of desperation was that most of us don't know what to do with our lives, and so we live this life much as if it a dress rehearsal for another life 'which will last forever.'"

Father John Powell (1989) "One third of all Americans wake up depressed every day. Professionals estimate that only 10 to 15 percent of Americans think of themselves as truly happy."

Thomas Szasz (1920-) in *Second Sin* (1973): "Happiness is an imaginary condition, formerly attributed by the living to the dead, now usually attributed by adults to children, and by children to adults."

tion possible, particularly when institutionalized in the form of religious beliefs about an afterlife. However, optimism comes with a cost: the denial of our instinctual nature and hence the denial of reality.

Religious optimism compensates people for the sacrifices necessary for civilization and is at the core of what Freud termed the "universal obsessional neurosis of humanity" (1928, p. 126). Freud once explained that the place where a crystal is broken most clearly reveals its structure. He felt that we could best discover human nature by examining where it is cracked. This 'disease focus' became prevalent in our Western world over the past several decades, such that psychologists focused their attention on the diagnosis and treatment of pathologies, and paid little attention to health or happiness. Freud gave dominance to the animalistic id; contemporary terror management theorists gave dominance to the fear of death. Social and cognitive psychologists studied our biases, delusions, illusions, and errors.

"Hope is a waking dream." Aristotle

Optimism vs Pessimism: The Battle

Freud proposed that optimism is part of human nature, but only as a derivative of the conflict between instincts and socialization. He thought some individuals, especially the educated, did not need the illusion of optimism, but the masses were best left with their "neurosis" intact and the belief that God was a benevolent father who would protect and guide them through life and beyond. He felt that one of the reasons most people obey laws is because they fear hell. As these psychodynamic "beliefs" became widespread throughout North America, Freud's formula equating (religious) optimism and illusion had tremendous impact.

Although the mental health profession denied that pessimism was the health standard, most theorists pointed to the accurate perception of reality as the pinnacle of highest mental function: "The perception of reality is called mentally healthy when what the individual sees corresponds to what is actually there" (Jahoda, 1958, p. 6). Psychologists and psychiatrists from the 1930's through the 1980's reflected these views in one form or another: Allport (1955), Erikson (1993), Fromm (1998), Maslow (1998), Menninger (1989) and Rogers (1995). "Reality testing" became the defining feature of the healthy, and the psychotherapists role was to expose people to reality, however painful it might be. Only modest expectations about the future could be considered realistic–anything more was seen as denial (Akhtar, 1996).

> **"Reality testing" became the defining feature of the healthy, and the psychotherapists role was to expose people to reality, however painful it might be.**

During the 1960s and 1970s, research evidence grew which showed that most people were neither realistic, nor accurate, in how they think. Cognitive psychologists documented shortcuts that people take as they process information. Marlin and Stang's (1978) meta-analysis of studies showed that language and memory are selectively positive. For example, in free recall, people produce positive memories sooner than negative ones and tend to always put a positive spin on their own memories of events. Most people evaluate themselves positively, particularly, more positively than they evaluate others.

Lazarus (1983) described what he called positive denial, and showed that it can be associated with well being following adversity. Beck (1967) developed his cognitive approach to depression and its treatment, the central core of which was the belief that depression was a cognitive disorder characterized by negative views about the self, experience, and the future; that is, by pessimism and hopelessness.

Taylor and Brown (1988) reviewed the literature on positive illusions, and showed that people are biased toward the positive, and that the only exceptions are anxious or depressed individuals. Taylor (1989) later posited that our tendency to see ourselves in the best light is a sign of well being. She distinguished optimism as an illusion, from optimism as a delusion: Illusions are responsive to reality, whereas delusions are not.

> **Optimism is an integral part of human nature, selected for in the course of evolution.**

"The art of being wise
is the art of knowing what to overlook."
William James

The strongest statement that optimism is an inherent aspect of human nature, is found in Tiger's (1979) *Optimism: The Biology of Hope*. Tiger felt that optimism is part of the biology of our species, and that it is one of our most defining and adaptive characteristics. He proposed that optimism is an integral part of human nature, selected for in the course of evolution, and even speculated that optimism drove human evolution. Once people began anticipating the future, they could imagine negative consequences, including their own mortality. Something had to develop to counteract the fear and paralysis that these thoughts might entail, and that thing was optimism. By this view, optimism is inherent in the makeup of people, not a derivative of some other psychological characteristic. So both optimism[12] and pessimism have enjoyed, or suffered, long and convoluted journeys to the present day.

Adler's (1910/1964,1927) fictional finalism, Lewin's (1935, 1951) field theory, and Kelly's (1955) personal construct theory provided influential frameworks for understanding how beliefs, both optimistic, pessimistic, guided people's behavior. Rotter's (1954, 1966) social learning theory and his generalized expectations of locus of control and trust legitimized broad expectancies about the future.

Psychology was becoming tired of traditional stimulus-response (S-R) approaches to learning and began replacing them with cognitive accounts (Peterson, Maier, & Seligman, 1993), that is, that our thinking controls our actions. We were no longer trapped in a black box; we could learn to get out. Hope emerged as a construct, but it was not to be studied for several more years.

Optimism began to appear in the literature with some regularity in the early 90's. Optimism is a mixed blend of emotions and

---

[12]In Scheier and Carver's (1992) self-regulatory model, dispositional optimism was termed as the expectation that good things will be plentiful and bad things, scarce. All areas of human behavior can be thought of in goal terms, and behavior involves the identification and adoption of goals, and the regulation of behavior to meet these goals. Seligman has approached optimism as an explanatory style: how we explain the causes of bad events can predict whether we become optimistic or pessimistic (Buchanan & Seligman, 1995). This notion of explanatory style developed from Seligman's earlier "learned helplessness" model (Abramson, Seligman, & Teasdale, 1978) in which animals and people who experienced uncontrollable aversive events learned to become unresponsive and by inference, helpless.

thoughts and beliefs that is still poorly defined.[13] Optimism has been linked to positive mood and high morale; to perseverance and effective problem solving; to academic, athletic, military, occupational, and political success; to popularity; to good health; and even to long life and freedom from trauma. Pessimism, on the other hand, is linked with depression, passivity, failure, social estrangement, morbidity, and mortality (Peterson, 2000). So it seems that the encouragement of healthy, realistic optimism would be a good thing.

Seligman added explanatory style to account for individual differences in response to uncontrollability. He felt that we have a customary way of explaining bad events–an explanatory style–and this style influences helplessness after adversity (Peterson & Seligman, 1984). Seligman (1991) reframed his theory from explanatory style to optimism in *Learned Optimism*, and more recently has become positively new age with his 2002 book *Authentic Happiness* which incorporates the recent trend (or fad) toward positive psychology.

One of the proponents of optimism and its powers is Csikszentmihalyi, who, during World War II, was struck by the resilience of some and the failure to adapt by others.

---

[13] Snyder (1994) studied the concept of hope in terms of our expectations that goals can be achieved. Hope was measured with a brief self-report scale (Snyder et al., 1996) with items such as "I energetically pursue my goals" and "There are lots of ways around any problem." Not surprisingly, high scores have been correlated with goal expectancies, perceived control, self-esteem, positive emotions, coping, and achievement (Irving, Snyder, & Crowson, 1998). Optimism has been connected to good health (Peterson, 1988; Peterson, Seligman, & Vaillant, 1988; Scheier & Carver, 1992) including immunological strength (Kamen-Siegel, Rodin, Seligman, & Dwyer, 1991; Scheier et al., 1999), absence of negative mood (Weisse, 1992), and health-promoting behavior (Peterson, Seligman, Yurko, Martin, & Friedman, 1998). Both the onset of disease (acted out through behavior and lifestyle choices) as well as the course of major illnesses such as AIDS or cancer may be predicted by optimism (Peterson, Moon, et al., 1998).

"As a child, I witnessed the dissolution of the smug world in which I had been comfortably ensconced. I noticed with surprise how many of the adults I had known as successful and self-confident became helpless and dispirited once the war removed their social supports. Without jobs, money, or status, they were reduced to empty shells. Yet there were a few who kept their integrity and purpose despite the surrounding chaos. Their serenity was a beacon that kept others from losing hope. And these were not the men and women one would have expected to emerge unscathed: They were not necessarily the most respected, better educated, or more skilled individuals. This experience set me thinking: What sources of strength were these people drawing on?" (Csikszentmihalyi, 2002)

There are activities that seem to satisfy our need to be optimistic but are pointless, psychological junk food. Are video games, the internet, mystery novels, gambling, and collections of various knick-knacks and do-dads just empty calories, whose pursuit consumes time and energy because they engage optimism, but eventually leave us with nothing to show?

SUMMARY

Societies are structured so that the great majority must believe that their well being depends on being passive and contented consumers. Their interest is to have the rest of the population depend on whatever rewards they have to offer.

101

If you buy the right car, the right vodka, or the right watch, we will guarantee your happiness, even if doing so will mortgage your life.

Psychiatry, in its concentration on repairing damage within a disease model, has neglected the fulfilled individual and the thriving community. The exclusive focus on pathology has resulted in a model of the human being lacking the positive features that make life worth living.

Optimism, and being 'positive,' have received bad press not only from psychology, but from most discplines who have not begun to re-think their heritage or consider their future.

In the following chapter, we examine the logical consequence of our worldview; creation of war and war-states.

Chapter Eight
War is a Four-Letter Word

Y ou do not have to enroll in Jewish History Crash Course #101 to understand the Spanish-American philosopher George Santayana's warning: "Those who cannot remember the past are destined to repeat it."

"War is an ugly thing, but not the ugliest of things. The decayed and degraded state of moral and patriotic feeling which thinks that nothing is worth war is much worse. The person who has nothing for which he is willing to fight, nothing which is more important than his own personal safety, is a miserable creature and has no chance of being free unless made and kept so by the exertions of better men than himself."
John Stuart Mill

People are losing their jobs. People in the middle-class are significantly poorer and have lost their savings through scandal and the market nosedive. Education and health care budgets are bankrupt. Services are being cut. The current emphasis on war and retribution conceals the failures of the administration at home, and upstages the faltering American economy.

Many believe that by not voting they are making a point about how they feel about the present state of politics. Younger people know that the differences between the two parties are so minute they're not making enough of a difference if they do vote. Historical experience indicates that the crucial element in changing policy is a national mass movement. In the civil rights movement, neither the Republicans nor the Democrats, including Kennedy and Johnson, were able or ready to end racial segregation in the South. It took the movement of African Americans in the South to force Congress to change. The Vietnam war ended under the Nixon administration, not under

Johnson. Both Republicans and Democrats had escalated the war, and mass protests ended the war. The history of the twentieth century–a hundred years

> **Sending messages to terrorists through violence leads to more terrorism.**

of retaliation, vengeance, war, terrorism and counter-terrorism, violence meeting violence, has created not peace but an unending cycle of stupidity."We shall make no distinction," said President Bush, "between terrorists and countries that harbor terrorists." Note similarities between Desert Storm (1990-1991) and the 2003- Iraqi war.[14]

That we commit terrorism to send a message to terrorists is analogous to a parent hitting a child to teach him a lesson about not

---

[14]**Chronology of Desert Storm (1990-91)**

1990	Hussein accuses Kuwait of oil overproduction and theft of oil
1990	US Ambassador to Iraq, April Glaspie, tells Hussien that the dispute is an Arab matter, not one that affects the United States.
1990	Hussein invades Kuwait. President Bush freezes Iraqi assets.
8-6-90	Economic sanctions are authorized.
8-7-90	Cheny visits Suadi Arabia. Fighter squadrons dispatched.
8- 8-90	Iraq annexes Kuwait.
8-9-90	The UN declares Iraq annexation invalid.
8-12-90	The USA announces interdiction program of Iraqi shipping.
8-22-90	President Bush authorizes call up of reserves.
9-14-90	Iraqi forces storm diplomatic missions in Kuwait City.
11-8-90	Bush orders additional deployments.
11-20-90	45 Democrats file suit in Washington to have President Bush seek Congressional approval of military operations (thrown out).
11-22-90	**President Bush visits the troops for Thanksgiving.**
11-29-90	UN Security Council authorizes force if Iraq does not withdraw from Kuwait.
1-12-91	Congress votes to allow for US troops to be used in offensive operations.
1-15-91	The deadline set by the UN Resolution 678 for Iraq to withdraw.
1-16-91	First statement of Operation Desert-Storm. "The liberation of Kuwait ..."

fighting with his siblings. It doesn't work. Reagan bombed Libya, and Bush bombed Iraq, Clinton bombed Afghanistan and a Sudanese pharmaceutical plant, to send a message to terrorists. Sending messages to terrorists through violence leads to more terrorism.

The Israeli-Palestinian conflict has taught us that car bombs planted by Palestinians result in air attacks and tanks by the Israeli government cause care bombs planted by Palestinians. It doesn't work. People all over the world resent America and American military action. A $300 billion dollar military budget does not give us security. Military bases all over the world, our warships on every ocean, have not given us security. Land mines and a "missile defense shield" will not give us security. We need to rethink our position in the world.

Fear of the U.S. government is based on the U.S. declared deter-

---

	US warplanes attack Baghdad and other military targets in Iraq.
1-17-91	Iraq launches first SCUD Missile attack.
1-30-91	US forces in the Gulf exceed 500,000.
2-13-91	US Bombers destroy a bunker complex in Baghdad with 300 civilians inside.
2-22-91	President Bush issues ultimatum for Iraqi troops to withdraw from Kuwait.
2-23-91	Ground war begins with Marines, Army and Arab forces moving into Iraq.
2-25-91	Iraqi SCUD missile hits a US barracks in Saudi Arabia, killing 27.
2-26-91	Kuwaiti resistance leaders declare they are in control of Kuwait City.
2-27-91	President Bush orders a cease fire effective at midnight Kuwaiti time.
3-3-91	Iraqi leaders formally accept cease fire terms
4-4-91	Ten Allied POWs freed
5-5-91	35 POWs released
3-8-91	First US combat forces return home.
4-6-02	Seventeen former prisoners of war file lawsuit to get Iraq pay damages for

torture. The lawsuit asks for $25 million in actual damages for each POW plus $5 million each to 21 family members and $300 million in punitive damages. According to published reports, Iraq has more than $1.7 billion in frozen assets in American banks. Congress reported that, if a judgment is made, payment may come from the frozen Iraqi assets. However, Congress now reports that these assets are being used to rebuild Iraq, specifically, to American companies who have been awarded contracts.

mination to rule the world by force, and to make sure that there will never be any challenge to that domination. Preventive wars can be fought at will: Preventive, not Pre-emptive. The U.S. can use military force to eliminate an imagined or invented threat. The goal is to prevent any challenge to the "power, position, and prestige of the United States." Such challenge, now or in the future, and any sign that it may emerge, will be met with overwhelming force by the rulers of the country that now outspends the rest of the world combined on means of violence, and is forging new and very dangerous paths over near-unanimous world opposition: development of lethal weaponry in space. The "imperial ambition" of the current power holders, has aroused fear around the world. The National Security Strategy declared that the U.S. alone had the right to carry out preventive war, using military force to eliminate a perceived threat, even if invented or imagined. (By the way, preventive war was the "supreme crime" that was condemned at Nuremberg).

The U.S. must alleviate the threats by paying more attention to *legitimate* grievances, and by agreeing to become a civilized member of a world community, with some respect for world order and its institutions. And this will be accomplished only by massive protests from the American people.

> *"Fear engenders cruelty; cruelty, fear, insanity,*
> *and then paralysis. In the center of Dante's circle,*
> *the damned remained motionless."*
> *Chris Hedges*

The instrument of empire is war and war is a poison–a poison that at times we must ingest, just as a cancer patient must ingest a poison to survive. But if we do not understand the poison of war–if we do not understand how deadly that poison is–it can kill us just as surely as the disease. War has become a spectator sport. The military and the press have turned war into a vast video arcade game. Its very essence–death–is hidden from public view.

"We make war that we may live in peace."
Aristotle, Nichomachean Ethics

Because we no longer understand war, we no longer understand that it can all go horribly wrong. We no longer acknowledge that war begins by calling for the annihilation of others, but ends–if we do not know when to make or maintain peace–with self-annihilation. We flirt, given the potency of modern weapons, with our own destruction.

> **Power exercised with ruthlessness can always crush others. But it doesn't always win.**

The seduction of war is insidious, because so much of what we are told about it is true–it *does* create a feeling of comradeship which obliterates our alienation and makes us, for maybe the only time in our life, feel we belong.

> "War allows us to rise above our small stations in life; we find nobility in a cause and feelings of selflessness and even bliss. And at a time of soaring deficits and financial scandals and the very deterioration of our domestic fabric, war is a fine diversion. War for those who enter into combat has a dark beauty, filled with the monstrous and the grotesque. The Bible calls it the lust of the eye and warns believers against it. War gives us a distorted sense of self; it gives us meaning."
>
> Chris Hedges

We Can Do Better

Power exercised with ruthlessness can always crush others. But it doesn't always win. Thucydides wrote about the war with Sparta that Spartan militarism in the short-term could conquer Athens. But that beauty, art, knowledge, philosophy, would outlive Sparta and Spartan militarism. Violence and force can win in the short-term. But in the long-term, it leaves only hollowness and emptiness. It does nothing to enrich our lives or propel us forward as human beings. War is a disease that infects and destroys individuals and societies. War dehumanizes the enemy. War is a drug that creates euphoria. Patriotism is narcissistic self-glorification that wow-we-can-inflict-violence.

> **War is a feverish video arcade game about cruise missiles hitting evil Iraqi planes, but nobody really gets hurt in the end. That myth boosts ratings, creates heroes, and sells magazines and newspapers.**

The media is part of the problem, and has been since the creation of the war correspondent. It's important for the nation and the state to unravel the positive spin of war, because it is difficult to get America to back war unless they believe in the glory and heroism myths. War is a feverish video arcade game about cruise missiles hitting evil Iraqi planes, but nobody really gets hurt in the end. That myth boosts ratings, creates heroes and sells magazines and newspapers.

With a book deal, multiple prime time interviews and a made for television movie under her belt, not to mention naked pictures of her frolicking with fellow soldiers in an army barracks safely stashed away in Larry Flynt's vault, the most famous soldier of the Iraq war–Private First Class Jessica Lynch–emerged as a result of the Positive Spin on war.

> MIAMI - Former Army Pfc. Jessica Lynch is to christen Carnival Cruise Lines' newest ship at Feb. 27 ceremonies in Jacksonville. Lynch will break a traditional bottle of champagne against the Carnival Miracle immediately preceding its three-day inaugural cruise from the Port of Jacksonville. She will be named the ship's 'god-mother.' "We are privileged that Miss Lynch, who represents thousands of courageous American men and women serving in our armed forces, has accepted our invitation to be god-mother," said Carnival President and CEO Bob Dickinson.
>
> The former supply clerk from West Virginia sustained broken bones and other injuries when her 507th Maintenance Company was ambushed in Nasiriyah, Iraq, on March 23. Her April 1 rescue from a hospital made her an instant celebrity, although she has disputed some of the more dramatic elements of her capture, including reports that she engaged in a fire fight with Iraqi soldiers.
>
> Carnival will make an undisclosed contribution to the Jessica Lynch Foundation, an organization that assists children of soldiers who have either served in the military or been killed on duty.
>
> NEW YORK - Reviews have been mixed and the facts are in question, but the authorized biogra-

phy of Pfc. Jessica Lynch is No. 1 on The New York Times' list of nonfiction best sellers.

"Clearly, people are responding to her story," said Paul Bogaards, of Alfred A. Knopf, which released *I Am a Soldier, Too* on Veteran's Day, written by former New York Times reporter Rick Bragg.

Lynch, a former supply clerk, sustained broken bones and other injuries when her 507th Maintenance Company was ambushed in Nasiriyah, Iraq, on March 23. Her rescue from an Iraqi hospital on April 1 made her an instant celebrity, although she has disputed some of the more dramatic elements. Lynch has said she was disturbed that the military seemed to overdramatize her rescue by U.S. troops, and spread false stories that she went down shooting in an Iraqi ambush.

Reviewing the book for the *Los Angeles Times*, Robert Scheer faulted Bragg for "his paltry investigation into the official mendacity that succeeded for a while in turning Lynch into a propaganda tool for a war that has been difficult to defend." Bragg, a Pulitzer Prize winning reporter, resigned from *The New York Times* last spring after the newspaper suspended him over a story that carried his byline but was largely reported by a freelancer. Lynch says she received a $1 million advance, while Bragg got $500,000. The Positive Spin pays off.

The ancient Greeks and Romans understood that war is a god, and that war always begins by calling for the annihilation of the other. But left unchecked, war always ends in *self-annihilation*. And in an age of apocalyptic weapons, we are beginning our own destruction. Going to war, any war, is always a step back; a failure for democracy, development and understanding. The foundations of world co-existence and international law were developed after two world wars precisely to prevent war. Are we deaf to the cries that have risen from all over the world, even from within our own country, to heed our lessons?

Let us remember our great responsibility before history, and use the enormous resources available to us to help humanity recover its faith in itself. We are silent in face of the torture of Robert Mugabe and his victims in Zimbabwe. We are silent when he committed his armed forces to a wasteful colonial-style intervention in the Congolese civil war which was filled with corruption, with government officials lining their pockets from Congo's rich mineral reserves while Zimbabwe's own economy plummeted out of control. We are silent throughout the oppression, torture and murder of those who oppose his regime. We are silent during the oppression of women throughout the world. The lesson we are teaching the world is that only economic interests, in this case oil and the war industry, can move us to take action and sow more violence, poverty, and hate around the world.

> "The last thing I want is that any of our descendents should look back in some years and despise us for not daring to act when we had so much capacity to act. We must dare to seek the how, the why and the what for of our agreements. We shall thus be able to join together to look for alternative solutions and new ways of managing the world's challenges. Being diverse is our richness, acting together will be our strength".
> Federico Mayor, Cancun Conference, 2 April.

ACTIONS

"Follow the path of the unsafe, independent thinker. Expose your ideas to the dangers of controversy. Speak your mind and fear less the label of 'crackpot' than the stigma of conformity. And on issues that seem important to you, stand up and be counted at any cost."
Thomas J. Watson

a) Read *Antigone*, when the king imposes his will without listening to those he rules or Thucydides' history. Read how Athens' expanding empire saw it become a tyrant abroad and then a tyrant at home. How the tyranny the Athenian leadership imposed on others it finally imposed on itself. This, Thucydides wrote, is what doomed Athenian democracy; Athens destroyed itself.

b) Stop sending weapons to countries that oppress other people or their own people.

c) Do not go to war, because war is terrorism.

d) Use our national wealth, not for guns, planes, bombs, but for the health and welfare of our people, for free medical care for everyone, guaranteed education and housing, fair wages and a clean environment.

Chapter Nine
Why Can't I Stay Miserable?
... or Why Happiness Matters

Aristotle stated that happiness is the whole aim and end of human existence. As we saw in Chapter One, most every culture ranks the pursuit of happiness as one of its most cherished goals (Diener & Oishi, 2000). Happiness has positive by-products, which benefit not only individuals, but families, communities, and societies (Myers, 1992). But will too much satisfaction will leave people unmotivated? Will pleasant emotions cause a shallow form of hedonism? Perhaps Dionysianism?[15]

Is there any value at all for any of us to work diligently toward real happiness? Is it worth the investment of the corporate world in helping to increase the happiness of their workforce? The evidence to date indicates that happy people *participate more in community organizations*, are *more liked by others*, are *less likely to get divorced*, tend to *live slightly longer, perform better at work* (Staw, Sutton, & Pelled, 1994), and *earn higher incomes* (Diener, Nickerson, Lucas, & Sandvik, 2000). Although these findings are correlational, and we have little understanding of 'why,' happy

---

[15] **Dionysus** was the most widely worshiped and popular god in ancient Greece. He was their god of wine, merriment, ritual dance, warm moisture, and later, civilization. He was often depicted as a handsome young man, dressed in fawn skin and carrying a goblet and an ivy-covered staff. After a complex set of events, Dionysus was turned into a goat by his father in an attempt to hide him from Hera. From then on he had small horns on his head. After he was safe, he went to live with the nymphs, who taught him to make wine. Hera eventually found him again, and this time she also warped his brain. The nymphs rejected him, and he went to live with the satyrs, who were men with goat legs and horns, and their leader Silenus. Dionysus traveled with the satyrs, who disgusted everyone they encountered with their rude, drunken behavior.

people *are* more productive and sociable. Thus, high levels of happiness might be beneficial for a society, and no evidence indicates they would be harmful. So, the old fear that if people get too content, they will slack off, seems not to hold water.

People with positive emotion are more flexible (Isen & Daubman, 1984), creative (Isen, Daubman, & Nowicki, 1987), integrative (Isen, Rosenzweig, & Young, 1991), open to information (Estrada, Isen, & Young, 1997), and efficient (Isen & Means, 1983; Isen et al., 1991). They show an increased preference for variety, and accept a broader array of behavioral options (Kahn & Isen, 1993).

Negative states such as anxiety, depression, and failure, predict narrow attention, whereas positive states such as subjective well-being, optimism, and success, predict broaden attention (Basso, Schelft, Ris, & Dember, 1996; Derryberry & Tucker, 1994). Personal resources built during states of positive emotions are durable and outlast the transient emotional states that led to their acquisition. These resources function as reserves that can be drawn on in less favorable emotional states.

Positive emotions are incompatible with negative emotions. You can't really hold both simultaneously; when you feel mixed emotions, they are just that–mixed. They are neither positive nor negative. This has been demonstrated in work on anxiety disorders (Wolpe, 1958), motivation (opponent-process theory; Solomon & Corbit, 1974), and aggression (principle of incompatible responses; Baron, 1976). If negative emotions are marked by increased cardiovascular activity, and this reactivity is implicated in cardiovascular disorders, positive emotions should undo this cardiovascular reactivity. Researchers have found that two types of positive emotions–mild joy and contentment–undo the lingering cardiovascular effects of negative emotions. Parasympathetic cardiac control may underlie positive emotions as well as the ability to regulate negative emotions (Fox, 1989; Porges, 1995).

People might improve their psychological well being, and perhaps their physical health, by cultivating experiences of positive emotions to cope with negative emotions. Resilient people 'bounce back' from stressful experiences quickly and efficiently" (Carver, 1998; Lazarus, 1993) and show faster cardiovascular recovery following negative emotion.

"Human beings, by changing the inner attitudes
of their minds, can change the outer aspects of their lives."
William James

Studies have shown that people who experience positive emotions during bereavement are more likely to create long-term plans and goals. Together with positive emotions, the existence of plans and goals predict greater psychological well being 12 months post-bereavement compared to those without plans and goals (Stein, Folkman, Trabasso, & Richards, 1997).

Emotions and Health

Healthy people are curious, vital, self-motivated, and inspired. They strive to learn, extend themselves, master new skills, and apply their talents responsibly. Happy, unhealthy people are very uncommon. Not only Westerners, but people of just about every culture have expressions, toasts, and clichés that reflect the high value that human beings place on health.

"He who has health has hope,
and he who has hope has everything."
Arab Proverb
"He who lacks health lacks everything."
French Saying
"Health is the first of all liberties."
Henri Amiel
"Health . . . is the first and greatest of all blessings."
Lord Chesterfield

Negative emotions are known to be toxic to human health and confiding self-disclosure has healing power (Pennebaker, 1990). Close, intact relationships predict health. Compared with those having few social ties, people supported by close relationships with friends, family, or fellow members of church, work, or other support groups are less vulnerable to ill health and premature death (Cohen, 1988; House, Landis, & Umberson, 1988; Nelson, 1988). Shelley Taylor and her collaborators argue that unrealistically optimistic beliefs about the future can protect from illness (Taylor et al., 2000). The results of numerous studies of patients with life-threatening diseases, such as AIDS, suggest that those who remain optimistic show symptoms later, and survive longer, than patients who confront reality more objectively. According to these authors, the positive effects of optimism are mediated mainly at a thinking level. An optimistic patient is more likely to practice habits that enhance health and to enlist social support. It is also possible, but not proven, that positive affective states may have a direct physiological effect that slows down the course of illness.

"We are what we repeatedly do."
Aristotle

116

Happiness increases when goals are:
• Intrinsic, concerned with community contribution, emotional intimacy, and personal growth *(Kasser & Ryan, 1996)*
• Congruent with one's motives and needs *(Sheldon & Elliot, 1999)*
• Feasible and realistic *(McGregor & Little, 1998; Oishi et al., 1999)*
• Valued by one's culture *(Cantor & Sanderson, 1999: Suh, 2000)*
• Not conflicting *(Emmons, 1986, 1996; Sheldon & Kasser, 1995).*

People appear to be happier when they:
• Choose to pursue success, rather than avoid failure *(Elliot & Sheldon, 1997)*
• Are highly committed to their goals *(Cantor & Sanderson, 1999)*
• Believe that they are making progress toward them *(Carver, Lawrence, & Scheier, 1996; Csikszentmihalyi, 1990).*

Happier people more likely have optimistic strategies in response to life's victories and defeats. These strategies include the tendency to:
• Frame life circumstances in positive ways *(DeNeve & Cooper, 1998)*
• Expect favorable life circumstances in the future *(Scheier & Carver, 1993; Seligman, 1991)*
• Feel control over one's outcomes *(Bandura, 1997; Grob, Stetsenko, Sabatier, Botcheva, & Macek, 1999)*
• Possess confidence about one's abilities *(Lyubomirsky & Lepper, 2000)*

Studies reveal greater well being among people who:
• Show positive illusions, that is, enhanced perceptions of themselves, their futures, and the extent of their control *(Armor & Taylor, 1998)*
• Derive positive meaning from negative events *(Folkman, 1997; McCrae & Costa, 1986; Taylor, 1983)*
• Use humour *(Nezu, Nezu, & Blissett, 1988)*
• Use spirituality and faith *(Myers, 2000)* in coping with adversity,
• Do not engage in repetitive, self-focused rumination *(Nolen-Hoeksema, Parker, & Larson, 1994)*
• Use social comparisons in useful ways *(Ahrens, 1991)*

Compared with those who are depressed, happy people are *less self-focused, less hostile and abusive*, and *less vulnerable to disease*. They also are *more loving, forgiving, trusting, energetic, decisive, creative, sociable,* and *helpful* (Myers, 1993; Veenhoven, 1988). Positive emotions are conducive to *sociability, optimistic goal striving,* even *healthy immune systems* (Weisse, 1992). They also define a kind of emotional background against which negative emotions, in response to threats, create louder signals. When something goes wrong, the 'stone in the emotional shoe' alerts us to take action. Those who are depressed, addicted, or overly anxious, having habituated to negative arousal, fail in their attempts to respond to negative emotional states.

Why are some people happy even during hard times? How come others are, even in the best of times, chronically unhappy, complaining, focusing on the negative and deriving little pleasure from life (Myers & Diener, 1995)? Evidence suggests that comparisons with how one's peers are doing (Diener & Fujita, 1997) with one's experiences in the past (Tversky & Griffin, 1991), and with one's desires and ideals (Carver & Scheier, 1998) influence whether the present makes one happy.

Remembering the negative aspects of events (Seidlitz & Diener, 1993) and dwelling and reflecting excessively on oneself and on one's problems (Lyubonursky, Tucker, Caldwell, & Berg, 1999) are not related to well being.

"I am a kind of paranoiac in reverse.
I suspect people of plotting to make me happy."
J. D. Salinger (1919 -)

Happy people are less sensitive to social comparison than unhappy people.[16] Unhappy people are deflated, rather than delighted, about their peers' accomplishments and triumphs, and are relieved rather than disappointed or sympathetic if their colleagues or acquaintances fail. Happy and unhappy people differ in how they distort social comparison information, how they use this information, and how they respond to it. Happy people see their abilities as more flexible than fixed, so that other people's exceptional performance is not a threat, but rather an incentive and an indication of their own possible future success. Happy people perceive, evaluate, and think about the same events in more positive ways than those who are unhappy. When such perceptions and experiences are repeated over a lifetime, happy and unhappy people preserve and promote their own happiness and unhappiness, respectively. Just as the "rich get richer" the happy get happier, and the unhappy get unhappier.

"Very little is needed to make a happy life."
Marcus Aurelius Antoninus (121 AD-180 AD), Meditations

Although happy people do more to protect their well being and self-esteem, they are less concerned with being happy (that is, managing their happiness) than unhappy people. Unhappy people dwell on themselves, their outcomes, and their moods, and are

---

[16]In one experiment, students solved puzzles next to a stooge who did the same task either faster or slower (Lyubomirsky & Ross, 1997). In another experiment, students received positive or negative feedback, and then heard someone else receive even more positive or even more negative feedback than they did. In both studies, everybody felt better when they heard their competitors did worse than they did; happy people didn't feel worse with others' superior performance. Unhappy students felt happier and more self confident when they received a poor evaluation but heard their competitor receive an even worse one, than when they received an excellent evaluation, but heard their peer receive an even better one.

more likely to dwell on negative or ambiguous events (Lyubomirsky et al., 2000).

"No man is happy who does not think himself so."
Publilius Syrus (100 BC), Maxims

Happy and unhappy people work to maintain or even increase their happiness and unhappiness. Happy people will choose to combine negative events and separate positive ones and to interpret a rejection or a setback as the cost of doing business.

Some people set goals to perceive the world in positive ways, that is, to appreciate themselves, to like other people, and to value the world at large, to be satisfied with what they have rather than focusing on what they do not have (Taylor & Brown, 1988). Others seem determined to perceive themselves, others, and the world around them in a realistic manner (i.e., to see things as they really are), and to maintain a consistent and accurate self-image. Chronically unhappy people do not want to reframe life events in positive and optimistic ways, or to avoid making comparisons with peers, or to cope with trauma through forgiveness and faith because they would rather be right than happy.

> **Chronically unhappy people do not want to reframe life events in positive and optimistic ways, or to avoid making comparisons with peers, or to cope with trauma through forgiveness and faith because they would rather be right than happy.**

Happy people may be more appealing marriage partners. Because they are more good-natured, more outgoing, and more focused on others (Veenhoven, 1988), they generally are socially attractive. Unhappy people are more often socially rejected. Misery may love company, but research on the social consequences of depression reveals that company does not love misery. An unhappy and thus self-focused, irritable, and withdrawn spouse or roommate is often not perceived as fun to be around (Gotlib, 1992; Segrin & Dillard, 1992). For such reasons, positive, happy people more readily form happy relationships.

> **Happy people may be more appealing marriage partners. Because they are more good-natured, more outgoing, and more focused on others, they generally are socially attractive.**

Because of recent research on the genetics of happiness, with heritability coefficients as high as 50 percent to 80 percent, some people suggest that 'trying to be happier' is as useless as 'trying to be taller' (Lykken & Tellegen, 1996, p. 189). However that might be valid, we find that our happiness can fluctuate within a set range; and our opportunity is to elevate levels toward the high point of the range. As with most genetic influences, we can intervene at the thought level.

SUMMARY

The old Puritan myth that happiness will lead to laziness or no good at all, as in, "the devil will find work for idle hands to do" or "idle hands are the devil's tools" seems to hold no evidence. In fact, those people who are happy report every possible benefit from good health to good relationships.

Although my comments on 'postive thinking' appear to be inconsistent with earlier remarks on the *danger* of positive thinking, the difference is this: optimism is very difference than positive thinking; it is an evaluation and interpretation of the evidence. Happiness involves optimism as a basis, with an overlay of other elements discussed in Chapters 11-13.

ACTIONS

If, because of your myths, or other secondary-gain maneuvers, you are dedicated to unhappiness, please re-read this chapter and evaluate whether it makes sense for you to hang onto these beliefs any longer. It is your choice.

Coming up in Chapter Ten, how our relationships and support systems actually do make us happier and live longer, and why this has become a challenge for us in the modern world.

Chapter Ten
With A Little Help from My Friends

"All human actions have one or more of these seven causes:
chance, nature, compulsion, habit, reason, passion, and desire."
Aristotle

Humans evolved in the context of small groups of around 50 to 200 people (Dunbar, 1993). Modern humans, in contrast, probably live in massive urban metropolis with millions of other humans. Ancestral humans may have had to choose from a dozen or two potential mates. Modern humans are surrounded by hundreds of potential mates, and thousands more through internet dating services. We are bombarded by media images of attractive models on a scale that has no historical precedent and that leads to unreasonable expectations about the quality and quantity of available mates.

Modern conditions of anonymity and isolated nuclear families deprive us of the social support of our ancestors (Nesse & Williams, 1994, p. 221). Today, kin members scatter in the pursuit of better jobs and promotions, yielding a social mobility that removes the social support of extended kin, and makes social bonds transient. If our well-being is dependent upon having deep intimate contacts, being a valued member of a social group, and being in a network of extended kin, then the conditions of modern living are designed to interfere with our happiness.

Thus, ancestral humans lived in extended kin networks, surrounded by uncles and aunts, nephews and nieces, cousins and grandparents. Modern humans live in isolated nuclear families devoid of extended kin. Ancestral humans relied on friends and relatives to seek justice, to correct social wrongs, and to deal with violence inflicted on them from others. Modern humans rely on police and a horrific legal system. These discrepancies between ancestral and modern environments create unanticipated psychological problems. Our brains have not adapted to keep up with all the changes (Koestler, 1990).

Benefits of Social Support

Among people with leukemia or heart disease, those who experience extensive social support have higher survival rates (Case, Moss. Case, McDermott, & Eberly, 1992; Colon, Callies, Popkin, & McGlave, 1991; Williams et al., 1992).

Following widowhood, divorce, or dismissal from a job, immune defenses weaken for a time, and rates of disease and death rise (Dohrenwend et al., 1982; Kaprio, Koskenvuo, & Rita, 1987). "Woe to one who is alone and falls and does not have another to help," observed the writer of Ecclesiastes (4:10).

> **People with increased social contacts and stronger support networks have lower premature death rates, less heart disease, and fewer health risk factors.**

Support Networks

Kindness cultivates connection. The heart can be our strongest muscle if we exercise it regularly. Support from family members and friends acts as a buffer against stress and illness. People with increased social contacts and stronger support networks have lower premature death rates, less heart disease, and fewer health risk factors. Some experts have concluded that the health benefits of social relationships may be as important as health risks such as smoking, physical inactivity, and high blood pressure. Social network size is consistently related to health and well being. Social networks provide both emotional benefits and actual assistance in time of need.

An individual's perception or awareness of the availability of support, regardless of the presence of a stressful circumstance, is health-enhancing.

Close Relationships

"We are told that people stay in love because of chemistry, or because they remain intrigued with each other, because of many kindnesses, because of luck . . . But part of it has got to be forgiveness and gratefulness."
Ellen Goodman.

Those who have close relationships cope better with stresses including bereavement, job loss, and illness (Perlman & Rook, 1987). Most people report being happier when attached than when unattached. Compared with those who never marry, and especially compared with those who have separated or divorced, married people report being happier and more satisfied with life.

> **Those who have close relationships cope better with stresses including bereavement, job loss, and illness.**

Among the 35,024 Americans surveyed by the National Opinion Research Center between 1972 and 1996, 40 percent of married adults declared themselves very happy–nearly double the 24 percent of never-married adults who said the same. Married people also have a decreased risk of depression.

Even less happy than those who are unmarried or divorced are those in unhappy marriages. However, those reporting their marriage as "very happy" are among the happiest: 57 percent reported life to be very happy compared with 10 percent of those whose marriage is "pretty happy" and three percent of those with an "unhappy" marriage. Married Americans say their spouse is their best friend, and four in five say they would marry the same person again (Glenn, 1996; Greeley, 1991).

The married versus not married happiness gap is similar for women and men from a meta-analysis of 93 studies of gender, marriage, and well-being (Wood, Rhodes, & Whelan, 1989). A bad marriage may be more depressing to a woman than to her husband, but single women are not happier than married women. So, is marriage conducive to happiness, or is happiness conducive to marriage?

Marital intimacy, commitment, and support pay emotional dividends. Marriage offers people new roles, providing new stresses but also additional rewards and sources of identity and self-esteem (Crosby, 1987). When marked by intimacy, marriage-friendship sealed by commitment reduces loneliness and offers a dependable lover and companion (Hendrick & Hendrick, 1997).

One of the most consistent findings in studies of well-being is the link to marriage (Diener et al., 1999). Married women and men are significantly happier than single women and men, even when other variables such as age and income are statistically controlled. Moreover, among married people, those who have succeeded in fulfilling their desire for a spouse who embodies the personality characteristics of agreeableness, conscientiousness, emotional stability, and openness to experience tend to be more emotionally and sexually satisfied with their marriages than those who fail to marry spouses with these qualities (Botwin, Buss, & Shackelford, 1997).

When two people are at one in their inmost hearts, they shatter even the strength of iron or bronze; and when two people understand each other in their inmost hearts, their words are sweet and strong like the fragrance of orchids.
Confucian and Taoist
source: I Ching

Aristotle recognized our role as social animals. Social bonds increased our ancestors' survival chances.

Aristotle recognized our role as social animals. Social bonds increased our ancestors' survival chances. Offspring kept close to their caregivers were protected from harm. Adults who attached, reproduced. Groups shared food, provided mates, and helped care for children. Facing enemies, there was strength in numbers. We have a deep need to belong (Baumeister & Leary, 1995).

Being attached to friends and partners with whom we can share intimate thoughts has two effects, believed Francis Bacon (1625): "It redoubleth joys, and cutteth griefs in half." John Lennon and Paul McCartney (1967) sang: "I get by with a little help from my friends." People report happier feelings when with others (Pavot, Diener, & Fujita, 1990). When asked by the National Opinion Research Center, "How many close friends would you say you have?" excluding family members, 26 percent of those reporting fewer than five friends and 38 percent of those reporting five or more friends said they were "very happy."

*"True happiness is of a retired nature, and an enemy to
pomp and noise; it arises, in the first place, from the
enjoyment of one's self, and in the next from the friendship
and conversation of a few select companions."*
Joseph Addison (1672 - 1719), The Spectator, March 17, 1911

According to (Myers, 1993; Myers & Diener, 1995), A satisfying
family life, intimate friends, time to reflect and pursue diverse
interests are what make us happiest.

Our relationships and our social interactions are a significant factor in how we gauge our own happiness, and also in how we rate
the happiness of others. One of the most enduring actions leading
to a deeper sense of joy, is in giving to others, or in the act of vol-
unteeering.

Volunteering

*"The essence of all art is to have
pleasure in giving pleasure."*
Mikhail Baryshnikov

Albert Schweitzer, Mahatma Gandhi, Martin Luther King, Jr.,
Mother Teresa, Aung San Suu Kyi in Burma, and Ken SaroWiwa
in Nigeria show that individuals can create a 'life theme' centered,
not only on personal and culture-specific challenges and goals,,
but also on concerns for other human beings, regardless of biological and cultural inheritance. Many ordinary people involved in
socially relevant careers have seen how this concern can be a
strong source of joy in their daily lives.

Life themes that are focused on jobs, challenges, or other goals are not less valuable or meaningful than are those with a larger scope. Everything we do can be performed from a strictly individual perspective or from a broader perspective of a global living system, whose elements share the same ecological niche and resources, the same biological structure and needs, and the same potentials for growth and development.

> *"Happiness is that state of consciousness which*
> *proceeds from the achievement of one's values."*
> *Ayn Rand (1905 - 1982)*

Volunteering helps individuals form interpersonal ties and develop their social networks. Social support is a key reason for the link between volunteering, life satisfaction, and health outcomes. While it is difficult to know whether healthy people are more likely to volunteer or whether volunteering provides health benefits, poor health was indicated as a barrier to volunteering by only 22 percent of Canadian non-volunteers recently surveyed in the National Survey on Giving, Volunteering and Participating (NGSVP).

> **Volunteering improves our quality of life and the health of our communities.**

Social participation may not only enhance the support available to individuals, but may also promote health by positively affecting thoughts, emotions, and behavior. Beyond the benefits of social ties gained from volunteer behavior, research by Young and Glasgow, among others, suggests a separate and distinct benefit of formal affiliation with community-oriented organizations. Volunteering provides opportunities to enhance employability, self-esteem, personal coping skills and resources, all of which have health benefits. The latest national study on volunteerism by the Gallup Organization found that 56 percent of American adults volunteer for community service; the Gallup study estimates in the order of 19.9 billion hours per year.

> *"The only true happiness comes from squandering ourselves for a purpose."*
> **William Cowper**

Benefits of Volunteering

Volunteering can improve our health. Volunteering is a great way to make friends, develop new skills and abilities, attain valuable employment experience, and broaden our perspective. It also improves the quality of life and the health of communities. Volunteer work improves the well being of individual volunteers primarily, but not exclusively, by enhancing social support networks.

SUMMARY

Ancestral humans lived in extended kin networks. Modern humans live in isolated nuclear families devoid of extended kin. Ancestral humans relied on friends and relatives to seek justice, to correct social wrongs, and to deal with violence inflicted on them from others. Modern humans rely on a horrific legal system. These discrepancies between ancestral and modern environments create unanticipated psychological problems.

In essence, the heart of happiness seems to open and bloom when we pursue an inspired purpose or mission in life–through both work and play–that fulfills our needs, challenges our skills, and assists others in meaningful ways.

ACTIONS

a)   Maintain greater emotional closeness to existing kin.

b)   Exploit electronic communication, including e-mail, phone, and video conferencing.

c)   Insist on the continued interaction of grandparents and grandchildren to strengthen the network of extended kin.

d)   Find a group or a cause and devote 10% of your time to it. Saying you are too busy is part of our sickness.

> *"Logotherapy...considers man as a being whose*
> *main concern consists in fulfilling a meaning*
> *and in actualizing values, rather than in the mere*
> *gratification and satisfaction of drives and instincts."*
> *Viktor E. Frankl, Man's Search for Meaning, p.164*

Chapter Eleven
Flow and Faith:
The Bases for Happiness

S o far we've seen that many life circumstances corre-
late with happiness at only modest levels, again supporting the idea of adaptation. For example, Campbell, Converse,
and Rodgers (1976) estimated that ten resources, including
income, number of friends, religious faith, intelligence, and education, together accounted for only 15 percent of the variance in
happiness. Campbell et al. and later investigators (e.g., Diener,
Sandvik, Seidlitz, & Diener, 1993) have found a small positive
correlation within countries between income and happiness. Rich
people, on average, are slightly happier than poor people (Diener,
Horwitz, & Emmons, 1985).

In a similar vein, Diener, Wolsic, and Fujita (1995) found that a
highly prized possession among college students, physical attractiveness, predicted only small amounts of variance in respondents' reports of pleasant affect, unpleasant affect, and life satisfaction. Perhaps even more striking, a number of studies showed
that objective physical health, even among the elderly, is barely
correlated with happiness (e.g., Okun & George, 1984). Two
basic attitudes toward life have been shown to form the basis–the
foundation–for a life of happiness; those are the capacity for
'flow,' and the growth of a strong spiritual base.

Flow

"Wheresoever you go,
go with all your heart."
Confucius

Mihaly Csikszentmihalyi (1990, 1999) observed increased quality of life when we use our skills in our work and our leisure activities. Between the anxiety of being overwhelmed and stressed and the apathy of being bored lies a zone in which people experience what Csikszentmihalyi terms flow. When their experiences are sampled using electronic pagers, people report greatest enjoyment –not when mindlessly passive–but when unself-consciously absorbed in a mindful challenge.

Pleasure vs Enjoyment

Pleasure is the good feeling that comes from satisfying homeostatic needs such as hunger, sex, and bodily comfort. Enjoyment, on the other hand, refers to the good feelings people experience when they break through the limits of homeostasis–when they do something that stretches them beyond what they were–in an athletic event, an artistic performance, a good deed, a stimulating conversation.

While watching television and hanging out with friends tend to be pleasurable for most teenagers (and many adults), if they become the main source of happiness, the teenager is likely to become an

---

Note. William James (1902/1958), Carl Jung (1936/1969), Gordon Allport (1961), and Abraham Maslow (1971), were interested in exploring spiritual ecstasy, play, creativity, and peak experiences, but these interests were eclipsed by medicalization.

134

adult who is limited in the ability to obtain positive experiences from a wide range of opportunities. Enjoyment, rather than pleasure, is what leads to personal growth and long-term happiness. So, why is that most people opt for pleasure over enjoyment? Why do people choose to watch television over taking on, and conquering, a challenging task, even when they know that their mental state while watching television is mild unhappiness (regardless of show content), whereas the task can produce joy? Asked how it felt when writing music was going well, a composer responded, "You are in an ecstatic state to such a point that you feel as though you almost don't exist. I have experienced this time and time again. My hand seems devoid of myself, and I have nothing to do with what is happening. I just sit there watching in a state of awe and wonderment. And the music just flows out by itself" (Csikszentmihalyi, 1975, p. 44).

> **Enjoyment, rather than pleasure, is what leads to personal growth and long-term happiness.**

This sense of 'having stepped into a different reality' can be induced by external events such as religious ceremonies, musical performances, or great films. The feeling can also be produced internally (and more reliably), by focusing attention on the pursuit of a meaningful goal. The composer claims that "you feel as though you almost don't exist." This dimension of the experience refers to involvement in the activity being so demanding, that no leftover attention remains. A pilot emerges from the cockpit after a grueling flight in turbulent, instrument conditions and can barely walk. The high energy and concentration required during the flight diminished the capacity of other parts of her body to respond, but she was unaware of this until she attempted to walk. Chess players stand up after a game and realize that they have terrible headaches and very full bladders. For hours during the game they had excluded information about their bodily states from consciousness.

An artist refers to the self-enhancing experience: "My hand seems devoid of myself ... I have nothing to do with what is happening." This sense of effortless performance is only possible because the skills and techniques have been learned and practiced so well that they have become automatic. One has to be in control of the activity to experience it, yet not try to consciously control what one is doing. As with any performance, including the performance of a professional speaker, when the conditions are right, action "just flows out by itself."

> "You lose your sense of time, you're completely enraptured, you are completely caught up in what you're doing, and you are sort of swayed by the possibilities you see in this work. If that becomes too powerful, then you get up, because the excitement is too great. The idea is to be so, so saturated with it that there's no future or past, it's just an extended present in which you are making meaning. And dismantling meaning, and remaking it." (Csikszentmihalyi, 1996, p. 121)

According to Csikszentmilialyi, another universal condition for the flow experience is that we feel our abilities to act match opportunities for action. If the challenges are too great for our skill, anxiety and inaction ensue; if the skills are greater than the challenges, we feel bored. When challenges are in balance with skills, we become lost in the activity and flow is likely to result (Csikszentmilialyi, 1975. 1997).

Creative activities, music, sports, games, and religious rituals are typical sources for self-enhancing experiences. Self-enhancers are those who have such experiences relatively often, regardless of what they are doing. We never do anything purely; our motives are usually mixed. Composers write music because they hope to sell it and pay the bills, because they want to become famous, because their self-images depend on writing songs. Volunteers travel to Mexico to work with the poor in clinics, not only because they feel good about themselves when they do (intrinsic reward), but because they like to be seen as giving and caring (extrinsic reward). If the composers and volunteers are motivated only by extrinsic rewards, they are missing the point. To write music or donate time for its own sake are the deeper rewards.

> **People are happy not because of what they do, but because of how they do it.**

People are happy not because of what they do, but because of how they do it. If they can experience joy working on the assembly line, chances are they will be happy. On the other hand, if they don't experience joy at a luxury spa, they are probably not going to be happy anywhere. The same is true of the various methods for becoming healthier: If the process is felt to be an external imposition, the technique is unlikely to lead to happiness. One must act on life, see oneself as the actor, and not the passive recipient of others' actions. People cannot "make us happy." We, alone, are responsible for our mental content, the activities or lack of them we choose, and the challenges we present to ourselves.

It seems that a prerequisite for happiness is the ability to get fully involved in life. If material conditions are abundant, so much the better, but lack of wealth or health need not prevent us from finding happiness in nearly any circumstance. Studies suggest that children from the most affluent families find it more difficult to be happy compared with less well-to-do teenagers. They tend to be more bored, less involved, less enthusiastic, and less excited.

It seems that a prerequisite for happiness is the ability to get fully involved in life.

One suggestion has been that more affluent teenagers experience joy less often because they spend less time with their parents, and they do fewer interesting things with them (Hunter, 1998). Nevertheless, joy alone does not guarantee a happy life. It is also necessary to find joy in activities that are complex; that is, activities that provide potential for growth over an entire life span, allow for the emergence of new opportunities, and stimulate the development of new skills.

Faith

"Hold faithfulness and sincerity as first principles."
Confucius, The Confucian Analects

Freud said religion was corrosive to happiness because it created an "obsessional neurosis" involving guilt, repressed sexuality, and suppressed emotions (1928/1964, p. 71). However, active religiosity is associated with several mental health criteria such as less delinquency, abuse of drugs and alcohol, divorce, and suicide (Batson, Schoenrade, & Ventis, 1993).

Perhaps because they smoke and drink less, religiously active people tend to be physically healthier and to live longer (Koenig, 1997; Matthews & Larson, 1997). Compared with religiously inactive widows, recently widowed women who worship regularly report more joy in their lives (Siegel & Kuykendall, 1990). Mothers of developmentally challenged children with a deep religious faith are less vulnerable to depression (Friedrich, Cohen, & Wilturner, 1988).

People of faith also retain or recover greater happiness after suffering divorce, unemployment, serious illness, or bereavement (McIntosh, Silver, & Wortman, 1993). In our later years, the two best predictors of life satisfaction are health and religiousness (Okun & Stock, 1987). Religiously active people report higher levels of happiness (Inglehart, 1990). In a Gallup (1984) survey, those with the highest scores on a spiritual commitment scale were twice as likely as those lowest in spiritual commitment to be "very happy." National Opinion Research Center surveys show higher levels of "very happy" people among those who feel "extremely close to God" (41 percent) rather than "somewhat close" (29 percent) or not close or unbelieving (23 percent). However, self-rated spirituality and happiness may both be socially desirable responses.

Religious communities provide social support (Ellison, Gay, & Glass, 1989), since religion is practiced communally, involving fellowship and sharing of burdens. The Amish, known for their agrarian, non-material culture, their pacifism, and their self-sufficient communal life, suffer low rates of major depression (Egeland & Hostetter, 1983).

The low depression rates and/or higher happiness self-ratings might result from the higher meaning and purpose that many people derive from their faith. Seligman (1988) feels that loss of meaning feeds today's high depression rate. Finding meaning requires an attachment to something larger than the self. To the extent that our young people find it hard to take their relationship with God seriously, to care about their relationship with the country or to be part of a large and abiding family, they find it difficult to find meaning in life. The self is a very poor site for finding meaning. Rabbi Harold Kushner (1987) thinks that religion satisfies "the most fundamental human need of all. That is the need to know that somehow we matter, that our lives mean something, count as something more than just a momentary blip in the universe."

Many religious worldviews not only propose answers to some of life's deepest questions; they encourage hope when confronting what Solomon, Greenberg, and Pyszczynski (1991) termed "the terror resulting from our awareness of vulnerability and death." Aware as we are of suffering and death, religion offers a hope that in the end, the very end, "all shall be well, and all shall be well, all manner of things shall be well" (Julian of Norwich, 1373/1901).

> *"If we cannot live so as to be happy,*
> *let us least live so as to deserve it."*
> *Immanuel Hermann Fichte*

There have been many very different ways to program the mind to increase happiness, or at least, to avoid being unhappy. Some religions promise that an eternal life of happiness follows our earthly existence. Others teach to give up desires altogether, and thus avoid disappointment. Still others, such as Yoga and Zen, have developed techniques for controlling the breath, and the stream of thoughts and feelings, thereby providing the means for shutting out negative content from consciousness.

Some of the most radical and sophisticated disciplines for self-control of the mind were those developed in India, culminating in the Buddhist teachings 25 centuries ago. Regardless of its truth content, faith in a supernatural order seems to enhance subjective well-being: surveys show a low but consistent correlation between religiosity and happiness (Csikszentmihalyi & Patton, 1997; Myers, 1993). Since that connection has been observed consistently, this chapter examines an alternative way of approaching religious thought with the intent to increase global optimism.

> **Many people live without reflection. Their lives may be full of activities without ever questioning or understanding why they do these things.**
> **They have no overriding structure or purpose to give meaning to the events of their lives, nor do they have a clear idea of their own nature or identity, of who they really are.**

Many people live without reflection. Their lives may be full of activities–they marry, have children, run a business, become executives–without ever questioning or understanding why they do these things. They have no overriding structure or purpose to give meaning to the events of their lives, nor do they have a clear idea of their own nature or identity, of who they really are.

Without spiritual meaning, we move through our brief life functioning on our most primitive level. That level, defined as everything we can perceive with our senses, is our survival level. In this level, we seek pleasure and try to avoid pain and suffering.

A Positive Spin

Our true nature is spiritual; life is an eternal process of spiritual discovery and growth. Beyond the physical body, each human has a soul, or a form of energy that cannot be created or destroyed and as such, continues to exist in another form after the death of the physical body. The development of the soul is the basic purpose of human existence.

Spiritual progress means acquiring the capacity to act in conformity with the Will of God (however that is defined) and to express the attributes and spirit of God in one's dealings with ourselves and with other human beings. The only true and enduring happiness for human beings lies in the pursuit of spiritual development.

> **Don't give up on God just because Sister Martha beat your fingers to a pulp; that was about *her*, not God.**

The fundamental role of religion is to enable people to achieve a true understanding of their own nature, and of God's will and purpose for them. The spiritual teachings set down by each system guide us to understanding the spiritual dynamics of life. If they teach only a set of rigid laws based on fear, and teach that only *their method* is the correct path to God, then they cannot be said to be spiritual. Don't give up on God just because Sister Martha beat your fingers to a pulp; that was about *her*, not God.

The ultimate aim in life of every human soul should be to attain moral and spiritual excellence–to align one's inner being and outward behavior with the will of an all-loving God. Each individual has been given a unique destiny that unfolds in accordance with the free exercise of the choices and opportunities presented in life.

Be generous in prosperity
Be thankful in adversity.
Be worthy of the trust of thy neighbor,
and look upon him with a bright and friendly face.
Be a treasure to the poor, an admonisher to the rich,
an answerer of the cry of the needy,
a preserver of the sanctity of thy pledge.

Be fair in thy judgment, and guarded in thy speech.
Be unjust to no man, and show all meekness to all men.
Be as a lamp unto them that walk in darkness,
a joy to the sorrowful, a sea for the thirsty,
a haven for the distressed, an upholder and
defender of the victim of oppression.

Let integrity and uprightness distinguish all thine acts.
Be a home for the stranger, a balm to the suffering,
a tower of strength for the fugitive.
Be eyes to the blind, and a
guiding light unto the feet of the erring.

Be an ornament to the countenance of truth,
a crown to the brow of fidelity,
a pillar of the temple of righteousness,
a breath of life to the body of mankind,
an ensign of the hosts of justice,
a luminary above the horizon of virtue,
a dew to the soil of the human heart,
an ark on the ocean of knowledge,
a sun in the heaven of bounty,
a gem on the diadem of wisdom,
a shining light in the firmament of thy generation,
a fruit upon the tree of humility.

CXXX Baha'u'llah p.285

The Pursuit of True Happiness is a Spiritual Quest

The purpose of this life on earth is for each of us to develop the spiritual and moral qualities that lie at the core of our highest nature. This requires a connection to an infinite source beyond oneself. No matter what you choose to call it, there is only one creator of the universe. From Abraham, Bah'ai, Krishna, Zoroaster, Moses, Buddha, Jesus, and Muhammad, throughout history a series of divine teachers have reflected the same truths presented in differing social contexts.

> **The purpose of this life on earth is for each of us to develop the spiritual and moral qualities that lie at the core of our highest nature.**

Good and evil are innate in the reality of man, and this is contrary to the pure goodness of nature and creation. The answer to this is that greed, which is to ask for something more, is a praiseworthy quality provided that it is used well. So, if a man is greedy to acquire science and knowledge, or to become compassionate, generous, and just, it is praiseworthy. If he does not use these qualities in a *right way*, they are negative. It is the same with all our natural qualities; if they are used and displayed in an unlawful way, they become 'wrong.'

Why Bother To Grow Spiritually?

One of the primary reasons to pursue spiritual development is that it helps us to develop qualities of faith, courage, love, compassion, trustworthiness, and humility, that lie at the foundation of human happiness and social progress. As these qualities are increasingly manifest, society as a whole advances.

144

"Happiness depends, as Nature shows,
Less on exterior things than most suppose."
William Cowper 1782

We have understood from the writings of Victor Frankl (1905-1997) and others, that we ourselves give meaning to our lives; life does not provide this meaning gratuitously (Frankl, 1963).

One way we become resilient in the face of adversity is by finding positive meaning in ordinary events and within adversity itself (Affleck & Termen, 1996; Folkman & Moskowitz, 2000; Fredrickson, 2000). The relation between positive meaning and resilience is reciprocal: Not only does finding positive meaning trigger resilience, but also positive emotions found in resilience increases the likelihood of finding positive meaning in subsequent events. Conversely, there is a downward spiral in which depressed mood and narrowed thinking influence one another reciprocally, over time leading to ever worsening moods and even clinical depression (Peterson & Seligman, 1984).

SUMMARY

Pleasure is the good feeling that comes from satisfying homeostatic needs such as hunger, sex, and bodily comfort. Enjoyment, on the other hand, refers to the joy that people experience when they do something that stretches them beyond what they were.

People are happy not because of what they do, but because of how they do it. Happy people create joy in their lives.

Faith is the creation of a belief that there is a meaning, a purpose, a higher end to life. Every faith is different in how this occurs. Some religions promise that an eternal life of happiness follows our earthly existence. Others teach to give up desires altogether. Still others provide the means for shutting out negative content from consciousness.

The ultimate aim in life of every human is to attain moral and spiritual excellence–to do what is meant. Each individual has been given a unique destiny that unfolds in accordance with the free exercise of the choices and opportunities presented in life.

ACTIONS

1. Examine the ratio of *flow to passive* activities in your life. Remember that the ruling classes are programming you to be passive recipients of their message that you are discontented and want more, and if you get it, you will be content. Do you waste your time leafing through people-and-event magazines, watching televison, and going to the movies? These *can* be worthwhile from time to time, but used as a substitute to life, they lead to emptiness and mass *ennui*.

2. Be open to exploring the role of spirutality in your life. Although religions attempt to form belief bases for spriutality, spirituality is not religion. Spirituality is a way of life.

In Chapter Twelve, we begin the exploration of a fundamental way of thinking that can lead to either joy or misery.

Chapter Twelve
Happiness: The Three Actions
"Life becomes real at the point of action."
Plato (204)

In the last chapter, we saw that it is not enough to 'think positively'–we must be *active on life*. To create meaning, we cannot passively receive enjoyment, but rather, commit to a task that stretches us beyond where we are now. Joy is found in our movement through the space between where we are, and where we need to be. Let's now explore how 'mental actions' form the core of authentic happiness.

We're not passive recipients of life. We personally interpret and remember life events through our interpretation. As such, two people in identical situations can experience a completely different subjective world. Happy people interpret life events in ways that maintain and promote their happiness and positive self-views, whereas unhappy individuals create experiences that reinforce their unhappiness and negative self-views. Happy individuals experience and react to events and circumstances in more positive and more adaptive ways. In what became the 'rose-colored glasses' hypothesis, Taylor and Brown (1988) suggested, that people were healthier if their sense of reality was biased in a positive direction. They found that healthier people overestimated their control on their environment, saw themselves in a positive light, and were unrealistically optimistic about the future.

"Most people are about as happy
as they make up their minds to be."
Abraham Lincoln

147

Some argue that optimistic and pessimistic people become that way by how they explain events to themselves. Seligman, Abramson, Peterson, and their colleagues have found that pessimistic style is linked to a higher risk of physical and mental disorders (Peterson, Seligman, & Valliant, 1988; Weisse, 1992). An optimistic explanatory style, in which people take credit for their successes and blame failures on specific external factors, is linked with better health and greater achievement. According to Peterson et al. (1998), people who were optimistic in childhood outlived their negative peers by almost two years.

> **We're not passive recipients of life. We personally interpret and remember life events through our interpretation. As such, two people in identical situations can experience a completely different subjective world.**

"The greatest discovery of my generation is that a human being can alter his life by altering his attitudes of mind."
William James

Some people say optimism is bad for you. In their studies of unrealistic optimism, Weinstein & Klein, 1996 have found that those who underestimate risk are less likely to take preventive action. For example, cigarette smokers may avoid thinking about, or trying to quit smoking by adopting biases that discount their own susceptibility to the risks of smoking. Those people who present an optimistic assessment of their emotional state by denying their negative emotions, even to themselves (Derakshan & Eysenck, 1999), tend to have significantly stronger physiological reactions to stress than those who are more realistic about their negative emotions.

Unrealistic Optimism

> *"The foolish man seeks happiness in the distance,*
> *the wise grows it under his feet."*
> *James Oppenheim*

When people are asked to provide an estimate of the likelihood that they will experience an illness or injury in the future, most underestimate their risks (Weinstein, 1989). We see ourselves as below average in risk for a variety of illnesses, which cannot, by definition, be true. This faulty belief inevitably leads us to neglect health mainte-

> **Optimism in the form of wishful thinking can distract us from making concrete plans about how to attain goals.**

nance. Optimism in the form of wishful thinking can distract us from making concrete plans about how to attain goals (Oettingen, 1996). Unrelenting optimism would prevent the caution and conservation of resources that usually accompany sadness as a normal and adaptive response to disappointment and setback (Nesse & Williams, 1996).

Constant striving for control over events, without the resources to achieve, can take a physical and mental toll if there is a real limit to what can be attained independent of hard work. If our society does not soon allow hard work to produce rewards, people will channel their efforts into unattainable goals and become ill and demoralized.

> *When there is room for doubt,*
> *fill the gap with hope.*

Thus, optimism is good for you if reality is not distorted; but although we are not very accurate in our assessments of reality, optimism by definition is probably realistic. There is a range of possible interpretations beyond which reality doesn't test out. We can choose to interpret anywhere along the continuum, from optimistic to pessimistic depending on which features we use to cause action. Realistic optimism involves hoping, aspiring, and searching for positive experiences–knowing that we do not know and accepting what we cannot know. Realistic optimism involves hoping for and working toward desired outcomes without having the expectation that those particular outcomes will occur.

> *"Ultimately, man should not ask what the meaning of his life is,*
> *but rather must recognize that it is he who is asked. In a word,*
> *each man is questioned by life; and he can only answer to life*
> *by answering for his own life; to life he can only respond by*
> *being responsible." Man's Search for Meaning, p.172*

There are three aspects to learning optimism, none of which are surprising or new.

1.　　Be lenient in our evaluation of past events.
2.　　Appreciate the positive aspects of current situation.
3.　　Routinely emphasize opportunities for the future.

> *"What the superior man seeks is in himself,*
> *the mean man seeks is in others."*
> *Confucius, The Confucian Analects*

Action One: Accept

Although optimism is usually associated with a positive outlook toward the future, we can also choose to evaluate past performances or events with an interpretation that focuses on the positive aspects. We always work at our highest possible

> We always
> work
> at our highest
> possible level.

level. I can conclude that I gave a good speech, or that my grandson played well in the soccer game–if there is some reasonable set of criteria on which to base those judgments and a lack of overwhelming evidence in opposition. Leniency (or compassion) means allowing a larger set of outcomes and events to be classified as subjectively positive–giving questionable outcomes and events the benefit of the doubt.

Search for positive aspects of a situation to neutralize or balance negative aspects. When realistic, leniency is not just pretending; rather it is discovering a perspective that is both truthful and favorable.

> *"Love it the way it is."*
> *Thaddeus Golas,*
> *Lazy Man's Guide to Enlightenment*

A reliable indicator of the ways in which you fail to accept yourself, is in your judgments of others. What do you find wrong with others? What do you most often criticize? Do you make suggestions for improvement? As you cut down your self-judgments, you notice a feeling of peace in your relationship with yourself, and with others (Lapp, 2002). When you accept yourself as an imperfect but OK being, you will inevitably accept others. We judge others to the degree that we judge ourselves. Have compassion; find what's right, be gentle with what's wrong; it usually corrects itself with love.

> *Focusing on the successful aspects of performance, even when success is only modest, is a form of shaping; it promotes positive emotion, reduces self-doubt, and maintains motivation.*
> *(McFarland & Ross, 1982).*

Acceptance, or the act of compassion, relies on flexible evaluations that help us accept less than ideal outcomes.

> *"We're here for a reason. I believe a bit of the reason is to throw little torches out to lead people through the dark."*
> *Whoopi Goldberg*

> *"When we honestly ask ourselves which person in our lives means the most to us, we often find that it is those who, instead of giving much advice, solutions, or cures, have chosen rather to share our pain and touch our wounds with a gentle and tender hand."*
> *Robin Sharma,Who Will Cry When You Die?*

Action Two: Appreciate

> *"Cherish all your happy moments:*
> *they make a fine cushion for old age."*
> *Christopher Morley (1890 - 1957)*

Be alert to positive aspects of your situation and feel thankful for what you have and for your circumstances. If we bring our attention to our current state, we can choose to focus on positive aspects of each situation and remind ourselves of the potential sources of good feelings that might otherwise pass unnoticed. Appreciation causes dishabituation. Routine people, places, things, and events that are usually taken for granted can be brought into awareness and acknowledged as important and positive contributors to one's positive experience. Appreciating what we like about our home, our family, and our job–and even about ourselves–promotes positive affect, more satisfying relationships and improved coping with stress (Affleck & Termen, 1996; Folkmam & Moskowitz, 2000).

Appreciation is especially important in long-term commitments or in difficult situations (Affleck & Termen, 1996). Research on decision-making has shown that people inflate the quality of an item they have chosen, compared to other options available for choice. Ashford and Kremer (1999) have suggested that workers transform the meanings attached to stigmatized jobs through recalibrating.

> **Appreciating what we like about our home, our family, and our job and ourselves, promotes positive emotion, more satisfying relationships, and improved coping with stress.**

That is, to find a reference point that increases satisfaction with the job and redirect attention to the better, rather than poorer, characteristics of the job. These same sorts of shifts in subjective values and attention have been found among those who are most satisfied with their marriage partner (Murray, 1999) and among those who have most effectively adjusted to traumatic events (Janoff-Bulman, 1989).

Action Three: Take Responsibility

"A man who becomes conscious of the responsibility he bears toward a human being who affectionately waits for him, or to an unfinished work, will never be able to throw away his life. He knows the 'why' for his existence, and will be able to

153

bear almost any 'how.'
Viktor E. Frankl, Man's Search for Meaning, p.127

Being realistic requires attention to both environmental and social feedback about whether beliefs fall outside the range of plausible (positive) possibilities. As Dr. Terry Paulson would say, "If one person calls you a horse's ass, ignore him; if four people call you a horse's ass, go buy a saddle." Self-deception is marked by the lack of attempts to gain reality checks. Self-deception relies on an active attempt to avoid information inconsistent with desired beliefs (Baumeister, 1996; Greenwald, 1997; Wright & Schneider. 1999). We deceive ourselves using stories we want to believe, for which we actively avoid reality checks. The child who has a magic ring, but refrains from using its magic, can continue to believe in its powers until tested.

> **Realistic optimism involves the search for environmental constraints and opportunities, whereas blaming relies on avoidance of information. Happy people are not blamers.**

"Things that are done, it is needless to speak about...
things that are past, it is needless to blame."
Confucius, The Confucian Analects

Chronic blaming has been linked to health problems (Termen & Affleck, 1990), and relationship difficulties (Fincham & Beach, 1999). The description of a criminal personality includes an 'unwillingness to take responsibility for self-initiated behaviors and a tendency to blame circumstances and others for negative outcomes related to their own transgressions' (Samenow, 1989).

One of the differences between criminal behavior and adaptive behavior, is the presence of active process to discover and alter changeable aspects of the environment. Realistic optimism involves the search for environmental constraints and opportunities, whereas blaming relies on avoidance of information. Criminals blame others because they want to avoid considering their own wrongdoing, not because they are motivated to discover the consequences of their behaviors.

The ability to take responsibility derives from a core belief that the only person who can change our life is ourself; not our spouse, our boss, or any of our external appearances. We all know this–but knowing and not practicing is not knowing. Think for a moment if you ever wish that others would change to suit you, if you ever feel resentful that others treat you the way they do; if you ever sense that you would be much happier, wealthier, more successful ... if the external events of your life had been or were different. It seems that where we place responsibility for our lives predicts our external success as well as our internal contentment. As Zimbardo stated succinctly: "A locus of control orientation is a belief about whether the outcomes of our actions are contingent on what we do (internal control orientation) or on events outside our personal control (external control orientation)" (Zimbardo, 1985, p. 275).

Some research (McCombs, 1991) suggests that what underlies the internal locus of control is the concept of 'self as agent.' This means that our thoughts control our actions, and that when we realize this executive thinking function, we can positively affect our beliefs, motivation, and performance. "The self as agent can consciously or unconsciously direct, select, and regulate the use of all knowledge structures and intellectual processes in support of personal goals, intentions, and choices" (p. 6). McCombs asserts that "the degree to which one chooses to be self-determining is a function of one's realization of the source of agency and personal control" (p. 7). In other words, we can say to ourselves, "I choose to direct my thoughts and energies toward accomplishment.." What is your locus of control? And what forces are responsible for your successes and failures? Find out with the Locus of Control Test in Appendix A.

SUMMARY

Happy individuals experience and react to events and circumstances in more positive and more adaptive ways. Acceptance, appreciation, compassion and responsibility are four virtues and actions that lie at the foundation of a satisfied and whole life.

ACTIONS

Based on the Three Actions, begin an action plan toward their mastery:

1.   Listen for your own judgments. Choose acceptance.

2.   Morning, noon and night, repeat what you appreciate. Force yourself to make appreciation statements concerning everything you see, touch, hear, and feel.

3.   Go easy on yourself. Interpret your behavior at its highest most compassionate level. If you could have done better, you would have. Next time.

4.   It is *not* easier to avoid life, to procrastinate, to continually excuse yourself from doing what you know you must. Take responsibility for the gifts you were given and exercise them.

In the following chapter, we'll work on the details of developing an optimistic approach to life, through which you can interpret events in a way that can lead to happiness.

Chapter Thirteen
Happiness: The Four Keys

Just as myths underlying the American belief system have led our society astray in the pursuit of false happiness, so too do our own basic belief systems. Many believe that to change a corporate culture, one must first adjust the basic beliefs or myths of that corporation (Lapp, 1996). In this chapter, we will expose the most common myths that create individual unhappiness.

No one wakes up in the morning and thinks, "I wish I was less happy." Consequently, it would seem that the path of happiness would be heavily traveled. But it's not as easy as it sounds, because many people embrace false ideas of what will actually create happiness in their lives. The most liberating of all realizations with regard to happiness is that, it's not what happens to us, but rather how we respond to what happens.

> **The most liberating of all realizations with regard to happiness is that it's not what happens to us, but rather how we respond to what happens that matters.**

The notion of "reconditioning" ourselves to be happy began with the ancient Stoics and was popularized by Albert Ellis (1994). Although many people blame external circumstances on their lack of happiness, experiences such as family problems, unsatisfying work, childhood traumas, a bad marriage, and all the other things we blame as the sources of our unhappiness, do not cause us to be unhappy. If we experience unhappiness, somewhere between the 'experiences' and our inter-

157

pretation, there is probably an irrational, self-defeating belief that is the actual source of our unhappiness. The consequences of these beliefs are negative emotions such as depression, panic, and rage.

> **Stop focusing on your inadequacy. These irrational beliefs result from your early conditioning from well-meaning people and institutions. Because you are biologically programmed to be susceptible to conditioning, you can condition yourself to believe differently.**

Although the original experiences may have caused real pain, it is our continuation of the same reaction we had then, to circumstances now, that perpetuates the feeling of unhappiness. For example, you feel like a 'loser' because you're not married, aren't dating, and believe that you will never find anyone. Yet, you are passionately involved with life, and have been extremely successful in most everything that you have done. You believe that it is absolutely necessary to have someone else in your life to depend on, and not to be in a unit is terrible and awful. With new evidence that it is not necessary to have a partner to be happy, you can stop focusing on your 'loser' status.

You feel sad because you erroneously think you are inadequate. Yet you perform just as well as others. With new evidence that you perform just as well as others, the belief that you are inadequate must be erroneous. *Stop focusing on your inadequacy.* These irrational beliefs result from your early conditioning from well-meaning people and institutions. Because you are biologically programmed to be susceptible to conditioning, you can condition yourself to believe differently.

Self-defeating beliefs tend to take the form of absolute statements. Instead of acknowledging a preference or a desire, you make demands on others, or convince yourself that you have an over-whelming need, which must be met. You may refuse to see that you do have some friends, or that you have had a few successes. You may dwell on and blow out of proportion the hurts that you have suffered. You may convince yourself that nobody loves you, or that you always screw up. We are very innovative and determined in our nyth creations.

For Ellis, these are the three main irrational beliefs:[17]

1.   "I must be outstandingly competent, or I am worthless."

a.   Do you beat yourself up for even the smallest mistake?

b.   Do you remember the negative things that happened to you, or that you said, and berate yourself for them?

c.   Do you find that it is never "enough?" You always feel you should have, could have, done more.

2.   "Others must treat me considerately, or they are absolutely rotten."

a.   Do you get miffed when people treat you poorly?

b.   Do you sometimes discard friends for minor infractions, saying "Well if that's the way you want to be, then ..."

3.   "The world should always give me happiness, or I will die."

---

[17] The complete Irrational Belief Scale with scoring can be found in the Appendix of this book, and is descibed in many sources including Malouff J.M., Schutte N.S., (Eds.) (1995). Irrational belief scale [IBS] (1986). *Sourcebook of adult assessment*. NY: Plenum Press, pp.432-435

a.   It is terrible when you have to be unhappy. It isn't fair.
b.   You expect that people should focus on your happiness, and help you out whenever possible.

The only treatment for these mental viruses is re-conditioning.

To do this, ask yourself:

1.   Is there any evidence *for* this belief?
2.   What is the evidence *against* this belief?
3.   What is the *worst* that can happen if I give up this belief?
4.   And what is the *best* that can happen?

Continual self-evaluation leads nowhere. The best thing for your health is to stop evaluating yourself altogether!

> **Continual self-evaluation leads nowhere. The best thing for your health is to stop evaluating yourself altogether.**

In our world of increasing terrorism, you don't need to keep terrorizing yourself with thoughts of responsibility for the terrorists. More and more people have been reporting the rise of a new set of over-generalized beliefs following 9-11, that if left unchecked could create a whole new set of difficulties:

For example: "I absolutely must be able to figure out a way to stop terrorists from acting so brutally and killing and maiming so many people, and there is something very inadequate about me because I can't find a way to stop this kind of terrorism."

These unrealistic and illogical overgeneralizations render people "unsane" (Korzybski, 1933). In the Ellis book, *Reason and Emotion in Psychotherapy,* all three of the above beliefs and other "shoulds" and "musts" can lead us not only to sadness with the terrorists' behavior (rational), but also to overwhelm ourselves with rage and depression (irrational). The first of these irrational beliefs will cause you to hate yourself for your weakness and inadequacy to stop terrorism. The second of these irrational beliefs will make you despise the terrorists and all other people who do cruel deeds, and consume yourself with rage. The third will make you hopelessly depressed about the present and future state of the world.

If we all keep reinforcing our irrational beliefs, we will simply enrage ourselves, encourage the terrorists to increase their fury, and encourage more retaliation until the cycle of retaliation precipitates a global war and the end of our planet.

Key #1: Love Begets Love

This section will sound similar to all those fluff books filled with gratuitous platitudes. These keys, however, have been developed consequent to research evidence, not to wishful thinking. Coincidentally, they are identical to those gratuitous platitudes! If you tend toward skepticism when reviewing these keys, it means that you are clinging to your need to be right rather than being willing to be happy. Success in these keys results from continual reconditioning practice, and it is possible.

Teach yourself and all others, unconditional self-acceptance. That is, fully accept yourself with all of your flaws and shadows. You can dislike your habits, and do your best to change your self-defeating behaviors and poor behavior toward others. This is a choice you make.

Unconditionally accept all other people as persons, no matter how badly they act. Some behaviors require sanctions and so be it. You can try to induce others to change their self-sabotaging and poor thoughts, feelings, and actions. In Christian terms, you unconditionally accept sinners but not their sins. This is a choice you make.

Unconditionally accept life, with its immense problems and difficulties, and teach yourself to have high frustration tolerance. This is a choice you make.

The theologian Reinhold Niebuhr (1892-1971) said it well:

"God grant me the serenity to accept the things I cannot change;
courage to change the things I can;
and wisdom to know the difference.
Living one day at a time;
Enjoying one moment at a time;
Accepting hardships as the pathway to peace;
Taking, as He did, this sinful world
as it is, not as I would have it;
Trusting that He will make all things right
if I surrender to His Will;
That I may be reasonably happy in this life
and supremely happy with Him
Forever in the next.
Amen.

In 1939, the prayer came to the attention of an early Alcoholics Anonymous member, who liked it so much that he brought it to Bill W., the co-founder of AA. Bill and the staff read the prayer and felt that it particularly suited the needs of AA. Cards were printed and passed around, and the simple little prayer became an integral part of the AA movement.

If you achieve these three philosophies; that is, unconditional self-acceptance, unconditional other-acceptance, and unconditional life-acceptance, will you be able to create world peace? Probably not. But, you will cope much better with terrorism, help others to cope with it, and model behavior that can eventually reduce terrorism to a minimum. This could take many of us many generations, but if we refuse to change our own belief systems for this long-term purpose, we will only insure renewed terrorism for decades or centuries until we self-annihilate.

> **This could take many of us many generations, but if we refuse to change our own belief systems for this long-term purpose, we will only insure renewed terrorism for decades or centuries until we self-annihilate.**

Love is the only force that can counter the force of death, and the death instinct.

The power of love empowers people to reconcile and forgive. A heart-warming example of love's power is the Muslim farmer who gave milk to a Serb baby for almost a year, even though his acts were reviled by his neighbors. The Serb couple whose baby had been saved could never denigrate Muslims the way their Serb neighbors could, because of that one act of love.

Every act of love, small or large, contains seeds of hope. That little child may grow up in the Serb part of Bosnia, where to this day there's terribly racist rhetoric against Muslims. And that child must know that she is alive because of a poor Muslim farmer whom she may never meet. We cannot underestimate these acts that often seem minimal and small in the face of war, but which are immensely powerful and give us hope.

"To survive as a human being is possible only through love. And when Thanatos is ascendent, the instinct must be to reach out to those we love, to see in them all the divinity, pity and pathos of the human. And to recognize love in the lives of others–even those with whom we are in conflict–love that is like our own."

> "It does not mean we will avoid war or death. It does not mean that we, as distinct individuals, will survive. But love, in its mystery, has its own power. It alone gives us meaning that endures. It alone allows us to embrace and cherish life. Love has the power both to resist in our nature what we know we must resist, and to affirm what we know we must affirm. And love, as the poets remind us, is eternal."
> Chris Hedges

Key #2: Defeat Means Begin Again

How we react to defeat–how we constantly adjust ourselves to the changing successes and failures we experience, and the attitude we take toward failures and mistakes–is the single most important factor separating the successful from the unsuccessful. When successful people fail, they think about what they can do differently the next time.

Seligman and his colleagues (1999, 2002) have studied the type of thinking required to stay on track emotionally and achieve success. Their studies began with animals and extended to a wide variety of groups, including depressed and non-depressed children and adults, successful and unsuccessful sports teams, including the NBA, successful and unsuccessful insurance salespersons, and others. They found that successful teams and satisfied non-depressed people reacted with the same kind of thinking to success and to failure, and unsuccessful teams and depressed people reacted with similar thinking. The secret, they feel, lies in the answer we give to these two questions that we always covertly ask ourselves:

> **If you are you measuring yourself with a yardstick that was custom-made for someone else, there will always be people who are better and worse than you are at everything.**

1.   **What caused this to happen?**
2.   **How predictable or stable is this success?**

Suppose that you are a travel agent calling the people on your warm lead list, and the 15th lead has just slammed the phone in your ear. Or imagine that you are an aspiring author with your 228th rejection notice in your hands, or you're making your fifth request for a Saturday night date. Your challenge is to keep going in these situations. Many quit. What is the key?

After a success, which is your reaction?

1.   **What caused this success?**
_✔_   "This was due to my hard work."
___   "I was lucky."

2.   **How predictable or stable is this success?**
        Is it expected to happen again?
_✔_   "This is something I usually do. I expected that."
___   "That was a fluke!"

After a *failure*, which is your reaction?

1.   **What caused this failure?**

_✔_   "The exam was very hard and I did not study enough."

___   " I blew it."

2.   **How predictable or stable is this failure?**
        Is it expected to happen again?

_✔_   "That is really not like me! Usually I do well."

___   "I never do well at anything."

Seligman and his colleagues have attributed this thought process as the difference between "mastery-oriented thinking" and "learned helplessness." When bad things happen, helpless people think failure is *internal* and *stable*, and mastery-oriented people think it is *external* and *changeable*. That does not mean that mastery-oriented people do not take responsibility for their actions. Rather, each failure turns into a renewed focus on how to change one's behavior to make things different.

"You are never going to get what you want out of life without taking risks. Remember everything worthwhile carries the risk of failure."
Lee Iacooca

"The greatest regrets I heard were not from those who had taken a risk and lost. Invariably, they felt proud for having dared, and even educated in defeat. The real regret, bordering on mourning, came from those who had not taken chances they had wanted to take and now felt it was too late."
Ralph Keyes, author of Chancing It

Key #3: Be Who You Are

If you are you measuring yourself with a yardstick that was custom-made for someone else, there will always be people who are better and worse than you are at everything. If I were a violin, how would I compare myself to a piano? Too small? If I was a Citabria acrobatic plane, how would I compare myself to a Citation jet? Too slow? They all have different purposes. Measure your growth with your own yardstick.

Ask yourself instead: "Am I a percentage ahead now in any area than I was last year? Last month?" Oliver Wendell Holmes tells us that "It is not the destination in life that is important–it is the direction in which we are traveling." Improvement works by small percentage increases.

1.   Are you trying to be happy? What do you in the pursuit of happiness rather than accomplishing other goals?
2.   Are you ever content with what you have, or do you always want what you do not have?

> **Ask yourself instead: "Am I a percentage ahead now in any area than I was last year? Last month?"**

Focus on what you have done, not on what you could have or should have done. Do not second-guess yourself. We always work at our highest possible level.

Key #4: You Can Make a Difference

Every individual has the capacity to make a difference. Allow reality to be depressing for a second, a fraction of a second, until it mobilizes an anger, which in turn mobilizes movement. There are good people everywhere who are deeply concerned about others and who are making a difference in our world. They are no different than you or me. The American History is replete with example.

William Penn, was an early colonist who made peace with the Delaware Indians instead of warring with them. John Woolman refused to pay taxes to support the British wars, and spoke out against slavery. Captain Daniel Shays, Revolutionary War veteran, led a revolt of poor Massachusetts farmers against oppressive taxes. John Ross was a Cherokee chief who resisted the removal of his people. Osceola was a Seminole leader imprisoned and killed for leading a guerrilla campaign against removal. Frederick Douglass better represented the struggle against slavery than did Lincoln. The great national movement of black and white abolitionists pushed a reluctant Lincoln into finally issuing a half-hearted Emancipation Proclamation, and persuaded Congress to pass the 13th, 14th and 15th Amendments. Woodrow Wilson insisted on racial segregation in federal buildings, bombarded the Mexican coast, sent an occupation army into Haiti and the Dominican Republic, brought our country into World War I, and put anti-war protesters in prison. Emma Goldman was one of those who Wilson sent to prison, and Helen Keller fearlessly spoke out against the war. John Kennedy began the covert war in Indochina, went along with the invasion of Cuba, and failed to act against racial segregation in the South. It was not until the people of the South took to the streets, endured beatings and killings, and aroused the conscience of the nation, that the Kennedy administration enacted the Civil Rights Act and the Voting Rights Act.

Fannie Lou Hamer was a Mississippi sharecropper, evicted from her farm and tortured in prison after she joined the civil rights movement. But she became an eloquent voice for freedom. Ella Baker counseled and guided young black people in the Student Nonviolent Coordinating Committee.

Our country is full of heroic people who are *not* presidents, military leaders, or financial wizards, but who are doing something to keep our spirit alive. There are continually courageous acts of ordinary people changing the world. An African-American woman named Rosa Parkes refused to sit at the back of the bus. A migrant worker named Cesar Chavez demanded that the immigrant workers be paid a living wage. Keith Meinhold, a gay naval officer told his story to the joint chiefs as they deliberate lifting the ban. Rosa Parks, Cesar Chavez, and Keith Meinhold never realized what their acts of courage would achieve, but today we live in a better world because of them. If you believe that there is nothing you can do as one person to change the world, remember these ordinary people who were simply following their beliefs. Each person counts, as we are giving, or being given to.

> **There are continually courageous acts of ordinary people changing the world.**

In the words of Mother Theresa:

"I never look at the masses as my responsibility. I look at the individual. I can love only one person at a time. I can feed only one person at a time. Just one, one, one.
So you begin–I begin. I picked up one person—maybe if I didn't pick up that one person I wouldn't have picked up 42,000.

The whole work is only a drop in the ocean.
But if I didn't put the drop in, the ocean
would be one drop less. Same thing for you,
 same thing in your family, same thing in the
church where you go. Just begin . . . one, one, one."

Kathy Kelly and Voices in the Wilderness, who, in defiance of federal law, have traveled to Iraq over a dozen times to bring food and medicine to people who suffered under the U.S.-imposed sanctions. Students on hundreds of college campuses are protesting their universities' connection with sweatshop produced apparel. At Wesleyan University students sat in the president's office for thirty hours until the administration agreed to all of their demands. In Minneapolis, there are the four McDonald sisters, all nuns, who have gone to jail repeatedly for protesting against the Alliant Corporations' production of land mines. Thousands have traveled to Fort Benning, Georgia, to demand the closing of the murderous School for the Americas.

We all know individuals–most of them unsung and unrecognized–who have, often in the most modest ways, spoken out or acted out their belief in a more egalitarian, more just, peace-loving society. To ward off alienation and gloom, it is only necessary to remember the unremembered heroes of the past, and to look around us for the unnoticed heroes of the present.

"We bear a moral responsibility in any situation to the extent
that we have the capacity to affect that situation."
Zinn

ACTIONS

a)   For one day, listen for your reactions to both positive and negative events. Compare them to the examples above.

b)   Challenge your reactions. Question whether or not they are true. If they are not, switch your thinking to mastery thinking. Sure, this takes discipline at first, but once you have the habit, it sticks.

c)   Replace the immediate response to making a mistake from anger to acceptance. When you do become angry with yourself, you reinforce the mistake by etching it in your mind, you prevent yourself from thinking and acting clearly.

d)   Stay the Course. Staying on track does not mean that you have to be perfectly on course all the time. Most of the time, you will probably be a little bit "off course." The key is to keep correcting. For example, if your risk is trying to lose weight, and you get off track and pig out, do not whip yourself, just correct and get back on track. Will Rogers says that even if you are on the right track, if you just sit there, you will get run over.

> **Do not look where you do not want to go or need to go. Do not listen to people who discourage you.**

To keep yourself going, keep a record of things you do right and complimentary things that people say about you. I still have my Grade One report card and occasionally read it. Even after all these years, it's encouraging to hear what my first teacher said about me. Do not look where you do not want to go or need to go. Do not listen to people who discourage you. Look down the hill to see how much you have accomplished, not up to the top to see how far you still have to go. People will criticize and discourage you, but consider the words of Ghandi: "They cannot take away our self-respect unless we let them."

And recall Eleanor Roosevelt's assertion that "No one can hurt you without your consent."

I wonder how this would translate at the societal level; if we could honor and support principles of love and acceptance at a global level. One solution might be the expanded acceptance of *Ubuntu* a Zulu word that articulates a world view, or vision of humanity. *Ubuntu* regards humanity as an integral part of eco-systems that lead to a communal responsibility to sustain life. Human value is based on social, cultural and spiritual criteria. Natural resources are shared on principle of equity among and between generations.

Chapter Fourteen begins the exploration of *Ubuntu* thinking.

Chapter Fourteen
Ubuntu: Hope for the World

So many gods, so many creeds,
So many paths that wind and wind,
While just the art of being kind
Is all the sad world needs
Ella Wheeler Wilcox, s.

How was it possible for South Africa to transform itself in so short a time, without a bloody revolution? How could Nelson Mandela, having spent 27 years in prison, lead his nation through change by calling for understanding and reconciliation? The answers may lie in an understanding of Ubuntu, both in impact on South Africa,[18] and what promise it may hold for the world.

Ubuntu is a Zulu word that articulates a world view, or vision of humanity. *Ubuntu* regards humanity as an integral part of eco-systems that lead to a communal responsibility to sustain life. Human value is based on social, cultural and spiritual criteria. Natural resources are shared on principle of equity among and between generations. *Ubuntu* means that people are people through other people. It also acknowledges both the rights and the responsibilities of every citizen in promoting individual and societal well-being. This unifying vision is expressed in the Zulu maxim:

---

[18]The South African Governmental White Paper on Welfare recognizes Ubuntu as: "The principle of caring for each other's well-being...and a spirit of mutual support. Each individual's humanity is ideally expressed through his or her relationship with others and theirs in turn through a recognition of the individual's humanity." (*Government Gazette*, 02/02/1996, No.16943, p.18, paragraph 18).

umuntu ngumuntu ngabantu translated as "a person is a person through other persons" or "I am what I am because of you." To be human is to affirm one's humanity by recognizing the humanity of others in its infinite variety of content and form.

At root, this phrase communicates basic respect, empathy and compassion for others. It describes a person as 'being-with-others' and prescribes what 'being-with-others' means.

> **At root, this phrase communicates basic respect, empathy and compassion for others. It describes a person as 'being-with-others' and prescribes what 'being-with-others' means.**

The *Ubuntu* philosophy applied to appropriate and acceptable government rule is one of generating agreement or building consensus. African Democracy is not simple majority rule; traditional African democracy operates in the form of discussions. While there is clear leadership, everyone speaks, and consensus can be built.

Zulu phrases *simunye* meaning "we are one" and "an injury to one is an injury to all" reinforce the community message. *Ubuntu* inspires us to open ourselves to others, to learn of others as we learn of ourselves. This respect for difference in others is central to *Ubuntu*. As such, *Ubuntu*'s respect for others is also a respect for individuality. Our Western concept of individuality expressed in the Cartesian maxim, "I think therefore I am" is the antithesis of *Ubuntu*. The individual in *Ubuntu* is not solitary, but defined in terms of his or her relationships to others. As relationships change, so do the individuals.

Ubuntu visualizes a community built upon interdependent relationships reflected in group work, or *shosholoza* meaning "work as one. This philosophy reflects in the almost one million stokvels in South Africa, collective enterprises, or cooperatives, in which making a profit is important, but never if it involves the exploitation of others. Profits are shared on an equal basis. As such, stokvels are based on the *Ubuntu* all encompassing world view of life and humanity.

Ubuntu is humanity towards others
"I am because you exist."

Ubuntu is the spirit and heritage of Southern African peoples that characterizes a way of being human. Ubuntu means to value the good of the community above self-interest, to strive to help others in the spirit of service, to show respect, and to be honest and trustworthy. It is mutual affirmation

> **"I think therefore I am"**
> **is the antithesis of**
> **Ubuntu. The individual**
> **in Ubuntu is not solitary,**
> **but defined in terms of**
> **his or her relationships**
> **to others. As relation-**
> **ships change, so do the**
> **individuals.**

and communal responsiveness. It is the self so rooted in the community, that personal identity is defined by what is given to the community.

"I am because we are, and since we are, therefore I am"
"It is through others that one attains selfhood."

Apartheid, the Afrikaans word meaning "apartness" was a system based on racial discrimination and segregation and was the state system of the government for South Africa between 1941 to 1990. To me, it symbolizes the growing separation of our world's com-

175

munities. Continued separation will bring our destruction, connection leads to peace and our salvation. Our role is to create ubuntu-based communities in the corporate world, our social worlds and in our own lives.

"But it won't work in the real world!?" In the South African province of KwaZulu-Natal, where Ubuntu is supposed to be part of every day life, violent ethnic and political clashes are frequent. How can this be, if their fundamental belief really does guide their behavior? Is Ubuntu possible in the real world? Amidst daily life in Soweto, a humane spirit reigns, one which characterizes people's allegiances and relations to one another.

The period of transition from 'colonial power' to 'independence' has not been painless in South Africa, nor has it been in any region throughout the world, including my native Quebec. Quebec and South Africa represent the only two truly bilingual 'nations' in the world. In South Africa, dissimilar to Quebec, poverty and disease have fueled wars and tribal conflicts, and have plagued the transition. Despite of this violent struggle, examples of African forgiveness and reconciliation abound. The non-violent transition of the South African society from a totalitarian state to a multi-party democracy, is not the result simply of political negotiation. It results from the emergence of an ethos of solidarity, a commitment to peaceful co-existence amongst South Africans despite their differences.

What impact do these two fundamental concepts of human individuality have on our society; our world?

In individualist societies, such as the United States, individualism usually translates into competitiveness for a perceived scarcity of goods. Individual interest rules, and others are regarded as a means to individual ends. Would an understanding and practice of *Ubuntu* impact our ability and capacity to foster peaceful, healthy communities? Would *Ubuntu* thinking be of value and have a positive impact in your workplace, your home, or your community?

Ubuntu inspires us to open ourselves to others, to learn of others as we learn of ourselves. How does this enable greater capacities for empathy towards another? How can *Ubuntu*'s "respect for the other's difference" contribute to resolving conflicts?

a)   Create a scenario of potential conflict that can take place any day, in your workplace, or your community: How the conflict came about, how it would develop and how it could end up. Use this scenario to discuss the differences between an *Ubuntu* approach and how things actually happen at work or in your community.

b)   What would the world look like based upon *Ubuntu*? Our new heroes are physicians, nurses, medical students, members of fire and police forces who save lives, whose first thoughts are not of violence, but healing, not of vengeance, but compassion. After the 9-11 attacks, we no longer felt alone; we connected with strangers, even with people we did not like. We belonged, wrapped in the embrace of the nation, the community; we no longer felt alienated. The danger of the external threat that comes when we have an enemy, is that it does not create friendship; it creates comradeship. And those in wartime are deceived about what they are undergoing. And this is why once the threat is over, once war ends, comrades often become strangers again.

In friendship, there is a deepening of our sense of self. We become, through the friend, more aware of who we are and what we are about; we find ourselves in the eyes of the friend. Friends probe, question, and challenge each other to make each of them more complete. With comradeship, the kind that comes to us in patriotic fervor, there is a suppression of self-awareness, self-knowledge, and self-possession. Comrades lose their identities in wartime for the collective rush of a common cause–a common purpose. In comradeship, there are no demands on the self. This is part of its appeal and one of the reasons we miss it and seek to recreate it. Comradeship allows us to escape the demands on the self that are part of friendship. In wartime, when we feel threatened, we no longer face death alone, but as a group. This makes death easier to bear. It does not lead to genuine connection.

> **And those in wartime are deceived about what they are undergoing. And this is why once the threat is over, once war ends, comrades often become strangers again.**

If we want to improve the human condition, it is not enough to help those who suffer. The majority of people also need examples and advice to reach a richer and more fulfilling existence.

GENERAL GUIDES

1. Enlarge The Scope Of The Future

If two individuals believe they will interact frequently in the extended future, they have a greater incentive to cooperate. If people know when the "last move" will occur, and that the relationship will end soon, there is a greater incentive for people to defect and not cooperate. Enlarging the scope of the future can be accomplished by making interactions more frequent and making a commitment to the relationship. Show your people the long view.

At home, this means a renewed focus on the higher level of the relationship; not that either of you will sacrifice yourself for it, but you will know that an entity called a relationship can nurture you and grow the common good for both of you. each time you are in conflict ask yourselves: "What is the best for the relationship?" In doing what is best for the relationship, you *ipso facto* do the best for yourselves.

> **Each time you are in conflict, ask yourselves: "What is the best for the relationship?" In doing what is best for the relationship, you do the best for yourselves.**

At work, develop a common vision for each department, each work-unit, each small gathering. "This is why we are here; this is our over-riding mission; this is the reason that we will sacrifice some of our individual goals and needs–because we know that in the end, the whole unit, including ourselves individually, will benefit."

2. Teach Reciprocity

Promoting reciprocity not only helps people by making others more cooperative, it also makes it more difficult for exploitative strategies to thrive. The larger the number of those who follow a tit-for-tat reciprocity strategy, the less successful it will be to attempt to exploit others by defecting. Essentially, the cooperators will thrive through their interactions with each other, whereas the exploiters will suffer because of a vanishing population of those on whom they can prey.

> *"Joyfully I give, with an attitude of abundance,*
> *for I know that as I give, I do receive."*

a)   Begin at home by building in regular acts of giving.

b)   Ask your children what they gave that day at school or amongst their friends. Create a family ritual of giving every day, and make notes of each others' giving acts. Create an overriding purpose in your family, a dedication or a mission of giving.

c)   Create the same vehicle of giving at work.

c)   Review three valuable and simple resources on Ubuntu at work.

Bhengu (1996). *Ubuntu: The essence of democracy,* Mbigi, L. (1995) *Ubuntu: The spirit of transformation management,* and Lapp, J.E. (2005, in press). *Ubuntu Leadership: New Hope for our World.*

Finally, join the Positive Spin Club at www.drjanetlapp.com for regular reminders, tips, notices and general encouragement. Hope and optimism emanate from knowledge, truth, and right action. I trust you will incorporate the knowledge from this book that suits you now and will be open to considering new information. Even though you might already have been aware of all the concepts explored in this book, my prayer and expectation is that you will take action now.

Appendix

SCALE	Pages
Depression Criteria	182
Anxiety Disorders	183
Satisfaction with Life Scale	184
General Happiness Scale	185
Gratitude Scale	186
IBI Scales	187-91
Social Network and Support	192-93
Locus of Control Scale	194-95

DEPRESSION

If you feel that you are suffering from depression, and not just periodic dark times that often accompany growth, or if you have thoughts of suicide, your depression can be treated with a combination of psychotherapy and perhaps an antidepressant medication.

Not all persons with depression will have all these symptoms or have them to the same degree. If you have four or more of these symptoms, if nothing can make them go away, if they last more than two weeks, and especially if you have thoughts of suicide, consult with a clinical psychologist or psychiatrist.

1. Persistent sad or "empty" mood.
2. Feeling hopeless, helpless, worthless, pessimistic and or guilty.
3. Substance abuse.
4. Fatigue or loss of interest in ordinary activities, including sex.
5. Disturbances in eating and sleeping patterns.
6. Irritability, increased crying, anxiety and panic attacks.
7. Difficulty concentrating, remembering or making decisions.
8. Thoughts of suicide; suicide plans or attempts.
9. Persistent physical symptoms or pains that do not respond to treatment.

ANXIETY DISORDERS

If you experiece any of these symptons, I would suggest that you consult a psychologist who is specially trained in cognitive-behavioral therapy.

1. **Generalized Anxiety Disorder** is characterized by excessive, unrealistic worry that lasts six months or more; in adults, the anxiety may focus on issues such as health, money, or career. In addition to chronic worry, symptoms include trembling, muscular aches, insomnia, abdominal upsets, dizziness, and irritability.

2. **Obsessive-Compulsive Disorder (OCD).** There are persistent, recurring thoughts (obsessions) that reflect exaggerated anxiety or fears; typical obsessions include worry about being contaminated or fears of behaving improperly or acting violently. The obsessions may lead an individual to perform a ritual or routine (compulsions)–such as washing hands, repeating phrases or hoarding–to relieve the anxiety caused by the obsession.

3. **Panic Disorder.** People with panic disorder suffer severe attacks of panic–which may make them feel like they are having a heart attack or are going crazy–for no apparent reason. Symptoms include heart palpitations, chest pain or discomfort, sweating, trembling, tingling sensations, feeling of choking, fear of dying, fear of losing control, and feelings of unreality.

4. **Social Anxiety Disorder (Social Phobia).**
Social Anxiety Disorder results in feelings of embarrassment in social or performance situations. Symptoms often come up in mid- or late adolescence. People have extreme anxiety about being judged by others or fear behaving in a way that might cause embarrassment. This anxiety may lead to avoidance behavior. Physical symptoms associated with this disorder include heart palpitations, faintness, blushing and profuse sweating.

5. **Specific phobias**. People with specific phobias have an intense fear reaction to a specific object or situation (such as spiders, dogs, or heights); the level of fear is usually inappropriate to the situation, and is recognized as being irrational. This can lead to the avoidance of common, everyday situations.

6. **Post-Traumatic Stress Disorder (PTSD).** PTSD can follow an exposure to a traumatic event such as a sexual or physical assault, witnessing a death, the unexpected death of a loved one, natural disaster or acts of terrorism experienced even indirectly. There are three main symptoms associated with PTSD: 'reliving' of the traumatic event (such as flashbacks and nightmares); avoidance behaviors (such as avoiding places related to the trauma), emotional numbing (detachment from others); and difficulty sleeping, irritability or poor concentration.

SATISFACTION WITH LIFE SCALE

Below are five statements that you may agree or disagree with. Using the 1-7 scale below, indicate your agreement with each item by placing the appropriate number on the line preceding that item.

7 = Strongly agree
6 = Agree
5 = Slightly agree
4 = Neither agree nor disagree
3 = Slightly disagree
2 = Disagree
1 = Strongly disagree

____   In most ways, my life is close to my ideal.
____   The conditions of my life are excellent.
____   1 am completely satisfied with my life.
____   So far, I have gotten the important things I want in life
____   If I could live my life over, I would change nothing.

____   **Total**

30-35   Extremely satisfied, much above average
25-29   Very satisfied, above average
20-24   Somewhat satisfied, average for American adults
15-19   Slightly dissatisfied, a bit below average
10-14   Dissatisfied, clearly below average
5-9   Very dissatisfied, much below average

Norms: Among older American adults, men score 28 on average and women score 26. The average North American college student scores between 23 and 25; eastern European and Chinese students on average score between 16 and 19. Male prison inmates score about 12 on average, as do hospital inpatients. Psychological outpatients score between 14 and 18 on average, and abused women and elderly caregivers (both surprisingly) score about 21 on average (Seligman, 2002).

184

GENERAL HAPPINESS SCALE

For each of the following statements and/or questions, please circle the point on the scale that you feel is most appropriate in describing you.

1. In general, I consider myself:

1	2	3	4	5	6	7
Not a very happy person						A very happy person

2. Compared to most of my peers, I consider myself:

1	2	3	4	5	6	7
Less happy						More happy

3. Some people are generally very happy. They enjoy life regardless of what is going on, getting the most out of everything. To what extent does this characterization describe you?

1	2	3	4	5	6	7
Not at all						Very much

4. Some people are generally not very happy. Although they are not depressed, they never seem as happy as they might be. To what extent does this characterization describe you?

1	2	3	4	5	6	7
Not at all						Very much

To score the test, total your answers for the questions and divide by 8. The mean for adult Americans is 4.8. Two-thirds of people score between 3.8 and 5.8.

Source: Lyubomirsky, S., & Lepper, H. S. (1999). A measure of subjective happiness: Preliminary reliability and construct validation. *Social Indicators Research, 46,* 137-155.

THE GRATITUDE SURVEY

Using the scale below as a guide, write a number beside each statement to indicate how much you agree with it.

1 = Strangly disagree	2 = Disagree	3 = Slightly disagree
4 = Neutral	5 = Slightly agree	6 = Agree
7 = Strongly agree		

_____1. I have so much in life to be thankful for.

_____2. If I had to list everything that I felt grateful for, it would be a very long list.

_____3. When I look at the world, I don't see much to be grateful for.

_____4. I am grateful to a wide variety of people.

_____5. As I get older, I find myself more able to appreciate the people, events, and situations that have been part of my life history.

_____6. Long amounts of time can go by before I feel grateful to something or someone.

Scoring Instructions

1. Add up your scores for items 1,2,4, and 5.
2. Reverse your scores for items 3 and 6. That is, if you scored a "7," give yourself a "1," ifyou scored a "6," give yourself a "2," etc.
3. Add the reversed scores for items 3 and 6 to the total from Step 1. This is your total score. This number should be between 6 and 42.

Based on a sample of 1,224 adults who recently took this survey as part of a feature on the Spirituality and Health website, here are some guidelines for making sense ofyour score (Seligman, 2002, p. 71).

If you scored 35 or below, then you are in the bottom one-fourth of the sample in terms of gratitude. If you scored between 36 and 38, you are in the bottom one-half of people who took the survey. If you scored between 39 and 41, you are in the top one-fourth, and if you scored 42, you are in the top one-eighth. Women tend to score higher than men, and older people score higher than younger people (Seligman, 2002).

IBI SCALES

Please enter the number that reflects how each sentence describes you most of the time. It is not necessary to think over any item very long. Mark your answer quickly, and then go on to the next statement. Be sure to answer all the statements. Mark how you actually think about the statement, NOT how you think you SHOULD think. Because you will be scoring your own assessment and nobody but you will see your responses.

Agree Disagree   Score   Statement

_____ _____ • _____ 1. It is important to me that others approve of me.
_____ _____ • _____ 2. I hate to fail at anything.
_____ _____ • _____ 3. People who do wrong deserve what they get.
_____ _____ •• _____ 4. I usually accept what happens philosophically.
_____ _____ •• _____ 5. If a person wants to, s/he can be happy under almost any circumstances.
_____ _____ • _____ 6. I have a fear of some things that often bothers me.
_____ _____ • _____ 7. I usually put off important decisions.
_____ _____ • _____ 8. Everyone needs someone s/he can depend on for help and advice.
_____ _____ • _____ 9. "A zebra can not change his/her stripes."
_____ _____ • _____ 10. I prefer quiet leisure above all things.
_____ _____ •• _____ 11. I like the respect of others, but I don't have to have it.
_____ _____ • _____ 12. I avoid things I cannot do well.
_____ _____ • _____ 13. Too many evil persons escape the punishment they deserve.
_____ _____ •• _____ 14. Frustrations do not upset me.
_____ _____ •• _____ 15. People are disturbed not by situations but by the view they take.
_____ _____ •• _____ 16. I feel little anxiety over unexpected dangers or future events.
_____ _____ •• _____ 17. I try to get irksome tasks behind me when they come up.
_____ _____ • _____ 18. I try to consult an authority on important decisions.
_____ _____ • _____ 19. It is almost impossible to overcome the influences of the past.
_____ _____ •• _____ 20. I like to have a lot of irons in the fire.
_____ _____ • _____ 21. It upsets me if people frown at me while I am speaking.
_____ _____ •• _____ 22. I don't mind competing in activities where others are better..
_____ _____ • _____ 23. Those who do wrong deserve to be blamed.
_____ _____ • _____ 24. Things should be different from the way they are.
_____ _____ •• _____ 25. I realize that I cause my own moods.
_____ _____ • _____ 26. I often can't get my mind off some concern.
_____ _____ • _____ 27. I tend to avoid facing my problems.
_____ _____ • _____ 28. People need a source of strength outside themselves.
_____ _____ •• _____ 29. Just because something once strongly affected your life, doesn't mean it always needs to.
_____ _____ •• _____ 30. I'm most fulfilled when I have lots to do.
_____ _____ •• _____ 31. I can like myself even when many others don't.
_____ _____ •• _____ 32. I like to succeed at something, but I don't feel I have to.
_____ _____ • _____ 33. Immorality should be strongly punished.
_____ _____ • _____ 34. I often get disturbed over situations I don't like.

187

____ _____ •• ____35. People who are miserable have made themselves that way.

____ _____ •• ____36. If I can't keep something from happening, I don't worry about it.

____ _____ •• ____37. I usually make decisions as promptly as I can.

____ _____ • ____ 38. There are certain people that I depend on greatly.

____ _____ •• ____39. People overvalue the influence of the past.

____ _____ •• ____40. I most enjoy throwing myself into a creative project.

____ _____ •• ____41. If others dislike me, that's their problem, not mine.

____ _____ • ____ 42. It is highly important to me to be successful in everything I do.

____ _____ •• ____43. I seldom blame people for their wrongdoings.

____ _____ •• ____44. I usually accept things the way they are, even if I don't like them.

____ _____ •• ____45. A person won't stay angry or blue long unless s/he keeps her/himself that way.

____ _____ • ____ 46. I can't stand to take chances.

____ _____ • ____ 47. Life is too short to spend it doing unpleasant tasks.

____ _____ •• ____48. I like to stand on my own two feet.

____ _____ • ____ 49. If I had had different experiences, I could be more than I am.

____ _____ • ____50. I'd like to retire and quit working entirely.

____ _____ • ____51. I find it hard to go against what others think.

____ _____ •• ____ 52. I enjoy activities for their own sake, no matter how good I am at them.

____ _____ • ____ 53. The fear of punishment helps people be good.

____ _____ •• ____ 54. If things annoy me, I just ignore them.

____ _____ • ____ 55. The more problems a person has, the less happy s/he will be.

____ _____ •• ____ 56. I am seldom anxious over the future.

____ _____ •• ____57. I seldom put things off.

____ _____ •• ____58. I am the only one who can really face my problems.

____ _____ •• ____59. I seldom think of past experiences as affecting me now

____ _____ •• ____60. Too much leisure time is boring.

____ _____ •• ____61. Although I like approval, it's not a real need for me.

____ _____ • ____ 62. It bothers me when others are better than I am at something.

____ _____ •• ____63. Everyone is basically good.

____ _____ •• ____64. I do what I can to get what I want and then don't worry about it.

____ _____ •• ____65. Nothing is upsetting in itself- only in the way you interpret it.

____ _____ • ____ 66. I worry a lot about certain things in the future.

____ _____ • ____ 67. It is difficult for me to do unpleasant chores.

____ _____ •• ____68. I dislike for others to make my decisions for me.

____ _____ • ____ 69. We are slaves to our personal histories.

____ _____ • ____ 70. I sometimes wish I could go to a tropical island and just lie on the beach forever.

____ _____ • ____ 71. I often worry about how much people approve of & accept me.

____ _____ • ____ 72. It upsets me if I make mistakes.

____ _____ • ____ 73. It's unfair that "the rain falls on both the just and the unjust."

____ _____ •• ____74. I am fairly easy going about life.

____ _____ • ____ 75. More people should face up to the unpleasantness of life.

____ _____ • ____ 76. Sometimes I can't get a fear off my mind.

____ _____ •• ____77. A life of ease is seldom very rewarding.

_____ _____ •• ____78. I find it easy to seek advice.
_____ _____ • ____79. Once something strongly affects your life, it always will.
_____ _____ • ____ 80. I love to lie around.
_____ _____ • ____ 81. I have considerable concern with how people are feel about me.
_____ _____ • ____ 82. I often become quite annoyed over little things.
_____ _____ •• ____83. I usually give someone who has wronged me a second chance.
_____ _____ • ____ 84. People are happiest when they have challenges and problems to overcome.
_____ _____ •• ____85. There is never any reason to remain sorrowful for very long.
_____ _____ •• ____86. I hardly ever think of such things as death and global war.
_____ _____ • ____ 87. I dislike responsibility.
_____ _____ •• ____88. I dislike having to depend on others.
_____ _____ • ____ 89. People never change, basically.
_____ _____ • ____ 90. Most people work too hard and don't get enough rest.
_____ _____ •• ____91. It is annoying, but not upsetting, to be criticized.
_____ _____ •• ____92. I'm not afraid to do things which I cannot do well.
_____ _____ •• ____93. No one is evil, even though his/her deeds may be.
_____ _____ •• ____94. I seldom become upset over the mistakes of others.
_____ _____ •• ____95. "Man makes his own hell within himself."
_____ _____ • ____ 96. I often find myself planning what I would do in different dangerous situations.
_____ _____ •• ____ 97. If something is necessary, I do it even if it is unpleasant.
_____ _____ •• ____ 98. I've learned not to expect someone else to be very concerned about my welfare.
_____ _____ •• ____ 99. I don't look upon the past with any regrets.
_____ _____ • ____ 100. I don't feel really content unless I'm relaxed & doing nothing.

SCORING THE IBI SCALES

ADD SINGLE DOT ITEMS: If the item has one dot [•] and you checked the *agree* box, give yourself 1 [one] point in the space provided next to the statement.

ADD DOUBLE DOT ITEMS: If the item has two dots [••] and you checked the *disagree* box, give yourself a point in the space provided next to the statement.

ADD up your points for the following items:

1. 11, 21, 31, 41, 51, 61, 71, 81, and 91   A= Total_____
2. 12, 22, 32, 42, 52, 62, 72, 82, and 92   B= Total_____
3. 13, 23, 33, 43, 53, 63, 73, 83, and 93   C= Total_____
4. 14, 24, 34, 44, 54, 64, 74, 84, and 94   D= Total_____
5. 15, 25, 35, 45, 55, 65, 75, 85, and 95   E= Total_____
6. 16, 26, 36, 46, 56, 66, 76, 86, and 96   F= Total_____

7. 17, 27, 37, 47, 57, 67, 77, 87, and 97   G= Total_____
8. 18, 28, 38, 48, 58, 68, 78, 88, and 98   H= Total_____
9. 19, 29, 39, 49, 59, 69, 79, 89, and 99   I= Total_____
10. 20, 30, 40, 50, 60, 70, 80, and 100   J=Total_____

Results:

A= The higher the total, the greater your agreement with the irrational idea that it is an *absolute necessity* for an adult to have love and approval from peers, family and friends.This blocks you when you try to please others *too much*, or do things simply because if you do you, you fear others will be disappointed or angry with you. Question this belief (it is not true, we do not need love and approval–we like it, but do not *need* it).

B= The higher the total, the greater your agreement with the irrational idea that you must be unfailingly competent and almost perfect in all you undertake.This might be high enough to prevent you from doing anything unless it's perfect and of course–it never is at first. So perhaps you avoid doing certain things altogether. And you are probably very hard on yourself, beat yourself when you don't do well. It is really hard to be as successful as you want to be if you keep this up. Tolerate mistakes, and stop getting mad at yourself.

C= The higher the total, the greater your agreement with the irrational idea that certain people are evil, wicked and villainous, and should be punished.This score might have more to do with global terrorism rather than personal blocks. But if there is any resentment toward anyone in your life, it is not helping you to stay attached to this. "The best revenge is living well."

D= The higher the total, the greater your agreement with the irrational idea that it is horrible when things are not the way you would like them to be.This belief takes a fairly high toll on us, things must be a certain way or it is very upsetting. Things are the way we want them to be very rarely. We aim toward a goal, we get close sometimes. And it is hard to let go of control. We care very much about it being right. Someone once said "There are many paths to the palace of wisdom."

E= The higher the total, the greater your agreement with the irrational idea that external events cause most human misery. They don't–people

190

simply react as events trigger their emotions.

F= The higher the total, the greater your agreement with the irrational idea that you should feel fear or anxiety about anything that is unknown, uncertain or potentially dangerous. Rethink the unknown as exciting rather than dangerous. It's the same emotion, just a different label. You will be safe.

G= The higher the total, the greater your agreement with the irrational idea that it is easier to avoid than to face life difficulties and responsibilities. Is there a slight tendency to avoid facing tough interactions, or conflict? Or wanting to escape the drudgery that goes along with success? Re-think this one!! Success and happiness are alwaus preceded by focused dedication.

H= The higher the total, the greater your agreement with the irrational idea that you need something other or stronger or greater than yourself to rely on. This is a familiar belief of many women, that we need to rely on experts, or that we are not ready, or that we are not enough on our own. Repeat often "I am enough, I have enough, I do enough."

I = The higher the total, the greater your agreement with the irrational idea that your past controls your behavior now, that if you were once hurt, you need to keep hurting, blaming and generally making yourself a victim. Just because something affected you once, the way you react to it is not frozen in stone. you have control over it. As long as you are blaming your past experiences, you are preventing yourself from taking control of our own future.

J= The higher the total, the greater your agreement with the irrational idea that happiness can be achieved by in action, passivity, and endless leisure. Success comes from hard work; we have to choose leisure *or* success. This work is often joyful, often exciting, but it is hard in that we need to keep focused, put in the hours, put in the effort. Happiness comes from focused work toward a goal. No other way.

Social Network and Support

This assessment is scored professionally. Howver, the questions can give you an idea of the components of a good social support network.

For Questions 1 - 3, choose from the following (please mark a-e):
a) none b) 1 - 2 c) 3 - 5 d) 6 - 9 e) 10 or more

1. How many relatives and friends do you have that you feel close to (relatives and friends that you feel at ease with, can talk to about private matters, can call on for help)?
Relatives _____ Friends _____

2. How many relatives or friends do you see at least once a month?
Relatives _____ Friends _____

3. How many people do you have in the area that you can readily count on for real help in times of trouble or difficulty, such as watching over children or pets, giving a ride to the hospital or store, or helping if you are sick?
Relatives _____ Friends _____

4. Do you belong to any of these groups? (Circle all that apply)
a) A social or recreational group?
Yes   No
b) A labor union, commercial group, professional organization?
Yes   No
c) Church or Religious group?
Yes   No
d) A group concerned with children? (PTA, Boy Scouts, etc.)
Yes   No
e) A group concerned with community betterment, charity service?
Yes   No
f) A support group or therapy group?
Yes   No
g) Any other group, with which you have regular contact?
Yes   No

5. How often do your close friends and relatives make you feel loved and cared for? Would you say: _____
a) Never
b) Rarely
c) Sometimes
d) Frequently
e) No need

f) Not applicable

6. How often are these friends and relatives willing to listen when you need to talk about your worries or problems? _____
a) Never
b) Rarely
c) Sometimes
d) Frequently
e) No need
f) Not applicable

7. How satisfied are you with the kind of relationship you have with your family and friends? Would you say: _____
a) Not at all satisfied
b) Not very satisfied
c) Somewhat satisfied
d) Very satisfied
e) Completely satisfied
f) Not applicable

8. Is there any one special person you know that you feel close and intimate with, someone you share confidences and feelings with, someone you feel you can depend on? Please circle: Yes   No

9. How often do you get together with this special person? _____
a) Daily
b) Weekly
c) Monthly
d) Several times a year
e) Once a year
f) Not applicable

10. How often do you feel that these friends and relatives make too many demands on you? Would you say: _____
a) Never
b) Rarely
c) Sometimes
d) Frequently
e) No need
f) Not applicable

11. Do you have children? Yes   No

Locus of Control

Julian Rotter (1966) devised a locus of control test to assess the extent to which an individual possesses internal or external reinforcement beliefs. For each of the items below, enter the letter that best describes your behavior or feelings, A or B. There are no right or wrong answers. This abbreviated survey will give you a general idea of where you stand on the locus of control personality dimension.

_____ 1.

A. Many of the unhappy things in people's lives are partly due to bad luck.

B. People's misfortunes result from the mistakes they make.

_____ 2.

A. In the long run, people get the respect they deserve in this world.

B. Unfortunately, an individual's worth often passes unrecognized no matter how hard he tries.

_____ 3.

A. I have often found that what is going to happen, will happen.

B. Trusting to fate has never turned out as well for me as making a decision to take a definite course of action.

_____ 4.

A. I like to explore a strange city or section of town by myself, even if it means getting lost.

B. I prefer a guide when I am in a place I don't know well.

_____ 5.

A. Becoming a success is a matter of hard work; luck has little or nothing to do with it.

B. Getting a good job depends mainly on being in the right place at the right time.

___ 6.

A. The average citizen can have an influence in government decisions.

B. This world is run by the few people in power, and there is not much the little guy can do about it.

___7.

A. When I make plans, I am almost certain that I can make them work.

B. It is not always wise to plan too far ahead, because many things turn out to be a matter of good or bad fortune anyhow.

___8.

A. As far as world affairs are concerned, most of us are the victims of forces we can neither understand, nor control.

B. By taking an active part in political and social affairs, people can control world events.

___9.

A. I enjoy spending time in the familiar surroundings of home.

B. I get very restless if I have to stay around home for any length of time.

___10.

A. It is hard to know whether or not a person really likes you.

B. How many friends you have depends upon how nice a person you are.

___11.

A. In the long run the bad things that happen to us are balanced by the good ones.

B. Most misfortunes are the result of lack of ability, ignorance, laziness, or all three.

___12.

A. I prefer friends who are excitingly unpredictable.

B. I prefer friends who are reliable and predictable.

Score 1 point for these responses (4, 9, and 12 are not scored).

1B	4 –	7A	10B
2A	5A	8B	11B
3B	6A	9 –	12 –

0-3	External locus of control (your fate determined by others)
4-7	Neither internal nor external (mid-point)
8-9	Internal locus of control (you control your own fate)

Index

Abundance 15, 47, 85, 180
Acceptance 155, 162-3, 171-2
Agape 35, 36
Age 42-6, 62, 74, 75
Alcohol 66-8, 138
Appreciation 152-3, 155
Aristotle 18, 25, 29, 30, 32, 44, 61, 72, 87, 91, 96, 107, 113, 123
Blaming 154
Csikszentmihalyi, M. 74, 84, 100-101, 117, 134-6, 141
Cultures: Collectivist 81
   Individualist 81
   Canada 16, 81, 86
   Germany 83, 85
   Japan 81, 83, 84
   Sweden 81,85
Declaration of Independence 17, 18, 25, 32, 35, 39
Depression 13, 14, 20, 47, 49, 60, 67, 85, 89, 92-3, 98, 100, 114, 121,
     125, 139, 140, 145, 157
Ellis, A. 157, 159-61
Faith 111, 117, 120, 133, 138-44, 145
Flow 84, 133, 134, 136, 146
Foreign Aid 16
Freud 94-6, 138
Health 18, 20, 43, 54, 61, 69, 76, 78, 82, 88, 96, 97, 100, 103, 112,
115-6, 121, 124-5, 129- 30, 133, 138-9, 148-9, 154, 160
Hedges, C, 106-8, 164
Hobbes, T., 26
Hume, D. 17
Irrational Beliefs 159
James, W. 32, 55, 98, 115, 136, 147
Jealousy 87-8
Jefferson, 27-9
Joy 15, 22-3. 55, 91-3, 115, 128, 135, 137-8. 143. 145-6
Leibniz, G.W. 25, 29, 30-31, 33
Locus of Control 155, 183
Locke, J. 18, 25, 26-7, 28, 30, 32, 33, 41, 56, 91
Lottery winners 39, 51-52
Love 22, 23, 25, 35, 37, 38-9, 93, 121, 125, 144, 161, 162-3, 164

Materialism 14,16, 19, 91, 55, 56
Marriage 42, 53, 121, 126-7, 152, 157
Media   21,23,26,42,59,60 67-75, 78-79, 108, 123
Money   14, 19, 44, 47, 49-55, 58, 61-2, 82, 90, 101
Obesity 54-55, 75-79
Optimism 16, 94, 96, 97, 98-9, 100, 102, 114, 141, 147-50, 158-60
Peace 38, 39, 86, 104, 107, 162-3, 168, 170, 176
Plato 29, 35, 91, 147
Pleasure 13-14, 18-19, 27, 35, 56-7, 91, 118, 128, 134-5, 145
Positive thinking 15, 94
Poverty 72-73, 84-6, 111, 176
Relationships 25, 28, 52, 60, 84, 116, 121, 123-4, 174, 17
Responsibility 31, 33, 61, 92, 111, 153-5, 160, 166, 169, 170, 172-3
Reversing Consequence Gradient 57
Seligman, M. 13, 47, 93, 99-100, 117, 139, 145, 148, 165-66
Smoking 66, 73-4, 79
Suicide 47, 81, 95, 138
Support Network 120, 124-5
Spirituality 142-45, 146
Szasz, T. 29, 66, 95, 91
Television 44, 60, 62,67,70,71,74,80,109,134,135
Vattel, E. 25, 31, 35, 36-8
Volunteering 128-130
Violence 66, 68, 69-71, 80, 177
War 103-9, 111, 112
Wealth   50-54, 61, 84
Weisel, E. 21
Work 14, 22, 39, 48-9, 52, 54, 57, 72, 86, 91, 105, 113-4, 116, 120,
        121, 130, 134, 136, 137, 149, 151, 153, 155, 157, 165, 167,
        170, 175-77, 199
Zimbardo, 155

References

Adams, M. (1998). *Sex in the Snow: Canadian Social Values at the End of the Millennium*. Toronto: Penguin Books Canada

Adams, M. (2000). *Better Happy Than Rich?: Canadians, Money, and the Meaning of Life*. Toronto: Penguin Books.

Adams, M. (2003). *Fire and Ice: The United States, Canada and the Myth of Converging Values*. Toronto: Penguin Books.

Adler, A. (1927). *The theory and practice of individual psychology*. New York: Harcourt, Brace & World.

Adler, A. (1964). Inferiority feelings and defiance and obedience. In H. L Argyle, M. (1986). *The psychology of happiness*. London: Methuen.

Affleck, G., & Termen, H. (1996). Construing benefits from adversity: Adaptational significance and dispositional underpinnings. *Journal of Personality, 64*, 899-922.

Alterman, E. (2003). *What Liberal Media? The Truth About Bias and the News*. New York: Basic Books.

Ahrens, A. H. (1991). Dysphoria and social comparison: Combining information regarding others' performances. *Journal of Social and Clinical Psychology, 10*, 190-205.

Allison, M. T. & Duncan, M. C. (1988). Women, work, and flow. In M. Csikszentmihalyi & I. Csikszentmihaiyi (Eds.). *Optimal experience. Psychological studies of flow at consciousness* (pp. 118-137). New York: Cambridge University Press.

Allport, G. W. (1961). *Pattern and growth in personality*. New York: Holt, Rinehart & Winston.

Argyle, M. (1999). Causes and correlates of happiness. In D. Kalmeman, E. Diener, & N. Schwarz (Eds.), *Well-being: The foundations of hedonic psychology* (pp. 353-373). New York: Russell Sage Foundation.

Ashby, F. G., Isen, A. M. & Turken, A. U (1999). A neuropsychological theory of positive affect and its influence on cognition. *Psychological Review, 106*, 529 550.

Ashby, F. G., Isen, A. M., & Turken, A. U. (1999). A neuropsychological theory of positive affect and its influence on cognition. *Psychological Review, 106,*529-550.

Bandura, A. (1997). *Self efficacy: The exercise of control*. New York: Freeman.

Baron, J. (1985). *Rationality and intelligence*. New York: Cambridge University Press.

Basso, M. R., Schefft. B. K., Ris, M. D., & Dember, W. N. (1996). Mood and local visual processing. *Journal of the International Neuropsychological Society, 2*, 249 255.

Benson, P. L.. Scales, P. C., Leffert, N., & Roeffikepartain, E. C. (19991, *A fragile foundation: The state of developmental assets among American youth*. Minneapolis. MN: Search Institute.

Beyer, R. (2003). *The Greatest Stories Never Told : 100 Tales from History to Astonish, Bewilder, and Stupefy.* New York: HarperResource.

Baumeister, R. F., & Leary, M. R. (1995). The need to belong: Desire for interpersonal attachment as a fundamental human motivation. *Psychological Bulletin, 117*, 497-529.

Baumeister, R. F. (1996). Self regulation and ego threat: Motivated cognition, self deception, and destructive goal setting. In P. M. Gollwitzer & J. A. Bargh (Eds.). *The psychology of action: Linking cognition and motivation to behavior* (pp. 27-47). New York: Guilford.

Beck, A. T. (1967). *Depression: Clinical, experimental, and theoretical aspects.* New York: Harper & Row.

Bentham, J. (1970). *An introduction to the principles of morals and legislation.* Darien, CT: Hairier. (Original work published 1789)

Benedikt, M. (1999). *Values.* Austin: The University of Texas Press.

Blumenthal, S. (2003). *The Clinton Wars.* New York: Farrar Straus & Giroux.

Boller, P. (1996) *Not So!: Popular Myths About America's Past from Columbus to Clinton.* NewYork: Oxford University Press.

Brickman, P.. Coates, D., & Janoff-Balman, R. (1978). Lottery winners and accident victims: Is happiness relative? *Journal of Personality and Social Psychology, 36,* 917-927.

Brickman, P., & Campbell, D. T. (1971). Hedonic relativism and planning the good society. In M. H. Appley (Ed.), *Adaptation-level theory* (pp. 287-305). New York: Academic Press.

Brown, L., Flavin, C., & French, H. (1998). *State of the world 1998.* Washington, DC: Worldwatch Institute.

Brown, D. (2003) *The da Vinci Code.* New York: Doubleday.

Brown, J. D. (1986). Evaluations of self and others: Self-enhancement biases in social judgments. *Social Cognition, 4,* 353-376.

Buchanan, G. M., & Seligman, M. E. P. (1995). *Explanatory style.* Hillsdale, NJ: Erlbaum.

Buchanan, G. M., & Seligman, M. E. P. (Eds.). (1995). *Explanatory style.* Hillsdale, NJ: Erlbaum.

Buss, D. M. (2000). *The dangerous passion: Why jealousy is as necessary as love and sex.* New York: Free Press.

Campbell, A., Converse, P. E., & Rodgers, W. L. (1976). *The quality of American life.* New York: Russell Sage Foundation.

Cantor. N., & Sanderson. C. A. (1999). Life task participation and wellbeing: The importance of taking pan in daily life. In D. Kahneman, E. Diener, & N. Schwarz (Eds.), *Well-being: The foundations of hedonic psychology* (pp. 230-243). New York: Russell Sage Foundation.

Carver, C. S. (1998). Resilience and thriving: Issues, models, and linkages. *Journal of Social Issues, 54,* 245-266.

Carver, C. S., & Scheier, M. F. (1998). *On the self-regulation of behavior.* New York: Cambridge University Press.

Carver, C. S., & Schiner, M. 1. (1990). Origins and functions of positive and negative affect: A control-prosizess view. *Psychological Review, 97,* 19-35.

Carver. C. S., Lawrence, J. W., & Scheier, M. F. (1996). A control-process perspective on the origins of affect. In L. L. Martin & A. Tesser (Eds.), *Striving and feeling: Interactions among goals, affect, and regulation* (pp. 11-52). Mahwah, NJ: Erlbaum.

Campbell, A. (1981). *The sense of well-being in America.* New York: McGraw-Hill.

Case, R. B., Moss, A. J., Case, N., McDermott, M., & Eberly, S. (1992). Living alone after myocardial infarction: Impact on prognosis. *Journal of the American Medical Association, 267,* 515-519.

Cohen, S. (1988). Psychosocial models of the role of social support in the etiology of physical disease. *Health Psychology, 7,* 269-297.

Colon, E. A., Callies, A. L., Popkin, M. K., & McGlave, P. B. (1991). Depressed mood and other variables related to bone marrow transplantation survival in acute leukemia. *Psychosomatics, 32,* 420-425.

Conason, J. (2003). *Big Lies: The Right-Wing Propaganda Machine and How It Distorts the Truth.* New York : Thomas Dunne Books.

Corn, D. (1996). *The Lies of George W. Bush: Mastering the Politics of Deception.* New York: Vintage.

Costa, P. T., McCrae, R. R., & Zondernian, A. B. (1987). Environmental and dispositional influences on well-being: Longitudinal follow-up of an American national sample. *British Journal of Psychology, 78,* 299306.

Cross, D (1997). *Pope Joan.* New York: Ballantine.

Crosby, F. J. (Ed.). (1987). *Spouse, parent, worker: On gender and multiple roles.* New Haven, CT: Yale University Press.

Csikszentriiihalyi, M. (1975). *Beyond boredom and anxiety.* San Francisco: Jossey-Bass

Csikszentmihalyi, M. (1990). *Flow: The psychology of optimal experience.* New York: Harper & Row.

Csikszentmihalyi. M. (1996). *Creativity, flow and the psychology of discovery and invention.* New York: HarperCollins.

Csikszentayihalyi, M. (1997). *Finding flow: The psychology of engagement with everyday life.* New York: Basicbooks.

Csikszentrnihalyi, M. (1999). If we are so rich, why aren't we happy? *American Psychologist, 54,* 821-827.

Csikszentrnihalyi, M.(2003) *Good business: Leadership, flow, and the making of meaning.* New York: Viking.

201

Daly, M., & Wilson, M. (1988). Homicide. Hawthorne, NY: Aldine.

Daly, M., Wilson, M., & Weghorst, S. J. (1982). Male sexual jealousy. Ethology and Sociobiology, 3, 11-27.

Diener, E., Emmons, R. A., Larsen, R. J., & Griffin, S. (1985). The Satisfaction With Life Scale. *Journal of Personality Assessment, 49,* 71-75.

Diener, E. Horwitz, J., & Emmons, R. A. (1985). Happiness of the very wealthy. *Social Indicators Research,* 16, 263-274

Diener, E., Sandvik, E., Seidlitz, L., & Diener, M. (1993). The relationship between income and subjective well-being: Relative or absolute? *Social Indicators Research, 28,* 195-223.

Diener, E. (1994). Assessing subjective well-being: Progress and opportunities. Social Indicators Research, 31, 103-157.

Diener, E., Wolsic, B., & Fujita, F. (1995). Physical attractiveness and subjective well-being. Journal of Personality and Social Psychology, 69, 120-129.

Diener, E., & Fujita, F. (1995). Resources, personal strivings, and subjective well-being: A nomothetic and idiographic approach. Journal of Personality and Social Psychology, 68, 926-935.

Diener. E.. Sub, E. K., Smith, IT, & Shan, L. (1995). National differences in reported well-being: Why do they occur? Social Indicators Research, 34, 7-32.

Diener, E. (1996). Subjective well-being in cross-cultural perspective. In H. Grad, A. Blanco, & J. Georgas (Eds.), Key issues in cross-cultural psychology (pp. 319-330). Liese, the Netherlands: Swets & Zeitlinger.

Diener, E., & Diener, C. (1996). Most people are happy. Psychological Science, 7, 181-185.

Diener, E., Suh, E. M., Lucas, R. E., & Smith, H. L. (1999). Subjective well-being: Three decades of progress. Psychological Bulletin, 125, 276-302.

Diener, E.. & Lucas, R. E. (1999). Personality and subjective well-being. In D. Kahneman, E. Diener, & N. Schwamz (Eds.), Well-being: The foundations of hedonic psychology (pp. 213-229). New York: Russell Sage.

Diener, E., & Suh, E. (1999). Societies we live in: International comparisons. In D. Kahneman, E. Diener, & N. Schwarz (Eds.), Well-being: The foundations of hedonic psychology (pp. 434-452). New York: Russell Sage Foundation.

Diener, E., Nickerson, C., Lucas, R. E., & Sandvik, E. (2000). The direction of influence between income and subjective well-being. Manuscript submitted for publication, University of Illinois at Urbana-Champaign.

Diener, E. (2000). Subjective well-being: The science of happiness and a proposal for a national index. American Psychologist, 55, 34-43.

Diener, E., & Suh, E. M. (Eds.). (2002). Subjective well-being across cultures. Cambridge, MA: MIT Press.

Diener, E., & Oishi, S. (2002). Income and subjective well-being across nations. In E. Diener & E. Suh (Eds.), Subjective well-being across nations. Cambridge, MA: MIT Press.

Derakshan, N., & Eysenck, M. W. (1999). Are repressors self-deceivers or other deceivers? *Cognition & Emotion, 13,* 1-17.

DeMoss, N.L. (2002) *Lies Women Believe: And the Truth that Sets Them Free* New York: Moody.

DeNeve, K. M. (1999). Happy as an extraverted clam? The role of personality for subjective well-being. *Current Directions in Psychological Science, 8,* 141-144.

DeNeve, K. M. & Cooper, H. (1998). The happy personality: A memanalysis of 137 personality traits and subjective well-being. *Psychological Bulletin, 124,* 197-229.

Derryberry, D., & Tucker, D. M. (1994). Motivating the focus of attention. In P. M. Neidenthal & S. Kitayama (Eds.), *The heart's eye: Emotional influences in perception and attention* (pp. 167-196). San Diego, CA: Academic Press.

Dohrenwend, B., Pearlin, L., Clayton, P., Hamburg, B., Dohrenwend, B. P., Riley, M., & Rose, R. (1982). Report on stress and life events. In G. R. Elliott & C. Eisdorfer (Eds.), Stress and human health: Analysis and implications of research. New York: Springer.

Dunbar, R. 1. M. (1993). Coevolution of neocortical size, group size, and language in humans. *Behavioral and Brain Sciences, 16,* 681-735.

Durham, W. H. (1991). *Coevolution: Genes, culture and human diversity.* Stanford, CA: Stanford University Press.

Estrada, C. A.. Isen, A. M., & Young, M. J. (1997). Positive affect facilitates integration of information and decreases anchoring in reasoning among physicians. *Organizational Behavior and Human Decision Processes, 72,* 117-135.

Easterbrook, G. (2003) *The Progress Paradox.* New York, Random House.

Easterlin, R. (1995). Will raising the incomes of all increase the happiness of all? *Journal of Economic Behavior and Organization, 27,* 35-47.

Egeland, B., Carlson, E., & Strafe, L. A. (1993). Resilience as process. *Development and Psychopathology, 5,* 517 528.

Ehrman, B.D.(Ed.) (2003).. *Lost Scriptures: Books that did not make it into the New Testament.* New York: Oxford University Press.

Ellison, C. G. (1991). Religious involvement and subjective well-being. *Journal of Health and Social Behavior, 32,* 80-99.

Ellison, C. G., Gay, D. A., & Glass, T. A. (1989). Does religious commitment contribute to individual life satisfaction? *Social Forces, 68,* 100-123.

Ellis, A. *(1994). Reason and Emotion in Psychotherapy,* New York: Birch Lane.

Elliot, A. J., & Sheldon, K. M. (1997). Avoidance achievement motivation: A personal goals analysis. *Journal of Personality and Social Psychology, 73,* 171-185.

203

Emmons, R. A. (1986). Personal strivings: An approach to personality and subjective well-being. *Journal of Personality and Social Psychology, 51,* 1058-1068.

Emmons, R. A. (1996). Striving and feeling: Personal goals and subjective well-being. In P. M. Gollwitzer & J. A. Bargh (Eds.). *The psychology of action; Looking cognition and motivation to behavior* (pp. 313-337). New York: Guilford Press.

Emmons. R. A., & King, L. A. (1989). Conflict among personal strivings: Immediate and long-term implications for psychological and physical well-being. *Journal of Personality and Social Psychology, 54,* 10401048.

Epicurus of Samos. (1998). Achieving the happy life. *Free Inquiry, 18,* 47-48.

Epicurus, (1993). *The essential Epicurus: letters, principal doctrines, Vatican sayings,* New York: Prometheus Books.

Estrada, C. A.. Isen, A. M., & Young, M. J. (1997). Positive affect facilitates integration of information and decreases anchoring in nat soning among physicians. *Organizational Behavior and Human Decision Processes, 72,* 117-135.

Felner, R. D., Brand, S., DuBois, D. L., Adan, A. M., Mulhall, P. F., & Evans, E. G. (1995). Socioeconomic disadvantage, proximal environmental experiences, and socioemotional and academic adjustment in early adolescence: Investigation of a mediated effects model. *Child Development, 66,* 774-792.

Fincham, F. D., & Beach, S. R. H. (1999). Conflict in marriage: Implications for working with couples. *Annual Review of Psychology, 50,* 47-77.

Folkmam S., & Moskowitz, J. T. (2000). Positive affect and the other side of coping. *American Psychologist 55,* 647 654.

Fox, N. A. (1989). Psychological correlates of emotional reactivity during the first year of life. *Developmental Psychology, 25,* 364-372.

Folkmam S. (1997). Positive psychological states and coping with severe stress. *Social Science Medicine, 45,* 1207-1221.

Folkman, S., & Moskowitz, J. T. (2000). Positive affect and the other side of coping. *American Psychologist, 55,* 647-654.

Frank, R. H. (1996). The empty wealth of nations. Unpublished manuscript, Johnson Graduate School of Management, Cornell University, Ithaca, New York.

Frankl, V. E. (1978). *The unheard cry for meaning.* New York: Simon & Schuster.

Fredrickson, B. L. (1998). What good are positive emotions? *Review of General Psychology, 2,* 300-319.

Fredrickson, B. L. (2000). Extracting meaning from past affective experiences: The importance of peaks, ends, and specific emotions, *Cognition and Emotion, 14,* 577-606.

Fredrickson, B. L. (2002). Positive emotions. In C. R. Snyder & S. J. Lopez (Eds), *Handbook of positive psychology.* New York: Oxford University Press.

Fredrickson, B. L., & Branigam C. (2002). Positive emotions. In T. J. Mayne St G. A. Baumann (Eds.), *Emotion; Current issues and future directions* (pp. 123-151). New York: Guilford Press.
Fredrickson, B. L., & Levenson, R. W. (1998). Positive emotions speed recovery from the car-diovascular sequelae of negative emotions. *Cognition and Emotion, 12,* 191-220.

Fredrickson, B. L., Maynard, K. E., Helms, M. J., Haney, T. L., Seigler,I Barefoot, J. C. (2000). Hostility predicts magnitude and duration of blood pressure response to anger. *Journal of Behavioral Medicine, 23,* 229 243.

Freedman, J. (1978). *Happy people: What happiness is, who has it, and why.* New York: Harcourt Brace Jovanovich.

Friedrich, W. N., Cohen, D. S., & Wilturner, L. T. (1988). Specific beliefs as moderator vari-ables in maternal coping with mental retardation. *Children's Health Care, 17,* 40-44.

Franken, A.(2003). *Lies and the Lying Liars Who Tell Them: A Fair and Balanced Look at the Right.* New York: EP Dutton.

Freud, S. (1964). *The future of an illusion.* London: Hogarth/Garden City, NY: Doubleday. (Original work published 1928).

Gallup, G. G., Jr. (1984, March). Commentary on the state of religion in the U.S. today. *Religion in America: The Gallup Report, No. 222.*

Gallup, G. G., Jr., & Newport, F. (1990, July). Americans widely disagree on what constitutes rich. *Gallup Poll Monthly,* pp. 28-36.

Geary, D. C., Rumsey, M., Bow-Thomas, C. C., & Hoard, M. K. (1995). Sexual jealousy as a facultative trait: Evidence from the pattern of sex differences in adults from China and the United States. *Ethology and Sociobiology, 16,* 355-383.

Gillham, J. E., Reivich, K. J., Jaycox, L. H., & Seligman, M. E. P. (1995). Prevention of depres-sive symptoms in schoolchildren: Two-year follow-up. *Psychological Science, 6,* 343-351.

Gilbert, P. (1989). *Human nature and suffering.* Hillsdale, NJ: Erlbaum.

Gilbert, D. T., Pinel, E. C., Wilson, T. D., Blumberg, S. J., & Wheatley, T. P. (1998). Immune neglect: A source of durability bias in affective forecasting. *Journal of Personality and Social Psychology, 75,* 617-638.

Greenberg, M. T., Lengria, L. J., Cole, J. D., & Pinderhughes, E. E. (1999). Predicting develop-mental outcomes at school entry using a multiple-fisk model: Four American communities. *Developmental Psychology, 35,* 403-417.

Greenwald, A. G. (1997). Self-knowledge and self deception Further consideration. In M. S. Myslobodsky (Ed.), *The mythomamias The nature of deception and self deception* (pp. 51-72). Hillsdale, NJ: ErIbaum.

Glenn, N. D. (1996). Values, attitudes, and the state of American marriage. In D. Popenoe, J. B. Elshtain, & D. Blankenhom (Eds.), *Promises to keep: Decline and renewal of marriage in America* (pp. 15-33). Lanham, MD: Rowman & Littlefield.

Gotlib, 1. H. (1992). Interpersonal and cognitive aspects of depression. *Current Directions in*

Psychological Science, 1, 149-154.

Greeley, A. (1992). *Faithful attraction.* New York: Tor Books.

Greenberg, M. T., Lengria, L. J., Cole, J. D., & Pinderhughes, E. E. (1999). Predicting developmental outcomes at school entry using a multiple-fisk model: Four American communities. *Developmental Psychology, 35,* 403-417.

Greenwald, A. G. (1980). The totalitarian ego: Fabrication and revision of personal history. *American Psychologist, 35,* 603-618.

Grob, A., Stetsenko, A., Sabatier, C., Botcheva, L., & Macels, P. (1999). A cross-national model of subjective well-being in adolescence. In F. D. Alsaker, A. Hammer, & N. Bodmer (Eds.). *The adolescent experience: European and American adolescents in the 1990s* (pp. 115-130). New York: Erlbaum.

Haring, M. J., Stock, W. A., & Okun, M. A. (1984). A research synthesis of gender and social class as correlates of subjective well-being. *Human Relations, 37,* 645-657.

Hart, C. (1996). *Secrets of Serotonin.* New York: St. Martin's Press.

Haselton, M. G., & Buss, D. M. (2000). Error management theory: A new perspective on biases in cross-sex mindreading. *Journal of Personality and Social Psychology, 78,* 81-91.

Hendrick, S. S., & Hendrick, C. (1997). Love and satisfaction. In R. J.Higgins, E. T. (1999). Self-regulation and quality of life: Emotional and non-emotional life experiences. In D. Kahmemarl, E. Diener & N Schwarz (Eds.), *Well-being: The foundations of hedonic psychology* (pp. 244-266). New York: Russell Sage Foundation.

House, J. S., Landis, K. R., & Umberson, D. (1988, July). Social relationships and health. *Science, 241,* 540-545.

Howard, L. (2003). *White Lies.* New York: Mira Books.

Huff, D. (1993). *How to Lie With Statistics.* New York: WW Norton.

Hurtig, M. (2002). *The Vanishing Country: Is It Too Late to Save Canada?* Toronto: McClelland & Stewart.

Hunter, J. (1998). The importance of engagement: A preliminary analysis. *North American Minnesotan Teachers' Association Journal, 23,* 58-75.

Inghilleri, P. (1999). *From subjective experience to cultural evolution.* New York: Cambridge University Press.

Inglehart, R. (1990). *Culture shift in advanced industrial society.* Princeton, NJ: Princeton University Press.

Inglehart, R. (1997). *Modernization and postmodernization: Cultural, economic, and political change in societies.* Princeton, NJ: Princeton University Press.

Irving, L. M., Snyder, C. R., & Crowson, J. J. (1998). Hope and coping with cancer by college women. *Journal of Personality, 66,* 195-214.

Isen, A. M. (1990). The influence of positive and negative affect on cognitive organization: Some implications for development. In N. Stein, B. Lzventhal, & T. Trabasso (Eds.), *Psychological and biological approaches to emotion* (pp. 75-94). Hillsdale, NJ: Erlbaum.

Isen, A. M. (2000). Positive affect and decision making. In M. Lewi, & J. M. Haviland-Jones (Eds.). *Handbook of emotions* (2nd ed., pp. 417-435). New York: Guilford Press.

Isem A. M., & Dauluman, K. A. (1994). The influence of affect on categorization. *Journal of Personality and Social Psychology, 47,* 1206-1217.

Isen, A. M., Daubman, K. A., & Nowicki, G. P. (1987). Positive affect facilitates creative problem solving. *Journal of Personality and Social Psychology, 52,* 1122 1131.

Isem A. M.. Johnson, M. M. S.. Mertz. E., & Robinson, G. F. (1985). The influence of positive affect on the unusualness of word associations. *Journal of Personality and Social Psychology, 48,* 1413-1426.

Isem A. M., & Means, B. (1983). The influence of positive affect on decision-making strategy. *Social Cognition, 2.* 18-31.

Isen, A. M., Rosenzweig, A. S., & Young, M. J. (1991). The influence of positive affect on clinical problem solving. *Medical Decision Making, 11,* 221 227.

Isen A. M., & Means, B. (1983). The influence of positive affect on decision-making strategy. *Social Cognition, 2,* 18-31.

Isen, A. M. (1984). Toward understanding the role of affect in cognition. In R. Wyer & T. Stull (Eds.), *Handbook of social cognition* (pp. 179-236). Hillsdale, NJ: Erlbaum.

Isen A. M.. Johnson, M. M. S.. Mertz. E., & Robinson, G. F. (1985). The influence of positive affect on the unusualness of word associations. *Journal of Personality and Social Psychology, 48,* 1413-1426.

Isen, A. M., Daubman, K. A., & Nowicki, G. P. (1987). Positive affect facilitates creative problem solving. *Journal of Personality and Social Psychology, 52,* 1122 1131.

Isen, A. M. (1990). The influence of positive and negative affect on cognitive organization: Some implications for development. In N. Stein, B. Lzventhal, & T. Trabasso (Eds.), Psychological and biological approaches to emotion (pp. 75-94). Hillsdale, NJ: Erlbaum.

Isen, A. M., Rosenzweig, A. S., & Young, M. J. (1991). The influence of positive affect on clinical problem solving. *Medical Decision Making, 11,* 221 227.

Isen, A. M. (1993). Positive affect and decision making. In M. Lewis & M. Haviland (Eds.), *Handbook of emotion* (pp. 261-267). New York: Guilford.

Isen A. M., & Dauluman, K. A. (1994). The influence of affect on categorization. *Journal of Personality and Social Psychology, 47,* 1206-1217.

Isen, A. M. (2000). Positive affect and decision making. In M. Lewi, & J. M. Haviland-Jones (Eds.), *Handbook of emotions* (2nd ed., pp. 417-435). New York: Guilford Press.

Ivins, M. & Dubose, L. (2003). *Bushwhacked: Life in George W. Bush's America.* New York: Random House.

Ito, T. A., & Cacioppm J. T. (1999). The psychophysiology of utility appraisals. In D. Kahneman, E. Diener, & N. Schwartz (Eds.), *Well being: The foundations of hedonic psychology* (pp. 470-488). New York: Russell Sage Foundation.

Izand, C. E. (1977). *Human emotions.* New York: Plenum.

Kahn, B. E., & Isen, A. M. (1993). The influence of positive affect on variety-seeking among safe, enjoyable products. *Journal of Consumer Research, 20,* 257-270.

Kahneman, D. & Tversky, A. (Eds.) (2000) *Choices, Values, and Frames.* Boston: Cambridge University Press.

Kahneman, D. Slovic, P., Tversky, A., & Tversky, A. (Eds.) (1982) *Judgment under Uncertainty*: *Heuristics and Biases.* Boston: Cambridge University Press.

Kahmeman, D. (1999). Objective happiness. In D. Kahneman, E. Diener, & N. Schwarz Hals). *Well-being: The foundations of hedonic psychology* (pp. 3-25). New York: Russell Sage Foundation.

Kahneman, D., Diener, E., & Schwarz, N. (Eds.). (1999). *Well-being: The foundations of hedonic psychology.* New York: Russell Sage Foundation.

Kahneman, D.(Ed), et al. (2003) Delusions of Success: How Optimism Undermines Executives' Decisions (*HBR OnPoint Edition*).

Kamen-Siegel, L., Rodin, J., Seligman, M. E. P., & Dwyer, J. (1991). Explanatory style and cell-mediated immunity. *Health Psychology, 10,* 229-235.

Kaprio, J., Koskenvuo, M., & Rita, H. (1987). Mortality after bereavement: A prospective study of 95,647 widowed persons. *American Journal of Public Health, 77,* 283-287.

Kasser. T., & Ryan, R. M. (1996). Further examining the American dream: Differential correlates of intrinsic and extrinsic goals. *Personality and Social Psychology Bulletin, 27,* 280-287.

Kasser. T. (1996). Aspirations and well-being in a prison setting. *Journal of Applied Social Psychologist, 26,* 1367-1377.

Kasser, T., & Ryan, R. M. (1993). A dark side of the American dream: Correlates of financial success as a central life aspiration. *Journal of Personality and Social Psychology, 65,* 410-422.

Kenrick, D. T., Gutierres, S. E., & Goldberg, L. (1989). Influence of erotica on ratings of strangers and mates. *Journal of Experimental Social Psychology, 25,* 159-167.

Kelly, G. A. (1955). *The psychology of personal constructs.* New York: Norton. 291.

Kim, D. D., & Lyubomirsky, S. (1997). Effects of unfavorable social comparisons on cognitive interference in happy and unhappy people.Unpublished honors thesis, Department of Psychology, University of California, Riverside.

Klerman, G. L., & Weissman, M. M. (1989). Increasing rates of depression. *Journal of the American Medical Association, 261,* 2229-2235.

Koenig, H. G. (1997). *Is religion good for your health? The effects of religion on physical and*

208

mental health. Binghamton, NY: Haworth Press.

Krugman, P. (2003). *The Great Unraveling: Losing Our Way in the New Century.* New York" WW Norton.

Kubovy, M. (1999). On the pleasures of the mind. In D. Kalmeman, E. Diener, & N. Schwarz (Eds.), *Well-being: The foundations of hedonic psychology.* (pp. 134-154). New York: Russell Sage Foundation.

Kushner, H. (1987, December). You've got to believe in something. *Redbook,* 92-94.

Lapp. J.E.(1996). *Plant your feet firmly in mid-air.* New York: Demeter Press.

Lapp, J.E. (2002). *Dancing wth Tigers.* New York: Demeter Press.

Lazarus, R. S. (1983). The costs and benefits of denial. In S. Benitz (Ed.). *Denial of stress* (pp. 1-30). New York: International Universities Press.

Lazarus, R. S. (1991). *Emotion and adaptation.* New York: Oxford University Press.

Lazarus, R. S. (1993). From psychological stress to the emotions: A history of changing outlooks. *Annual Review of Psychology, 44.* 1-22.

Lazarus, R. S., Kanner, A. D., & Folliman, S. (1980). Emotions: A cognitive-phenomenological analysis. In R. Plutchik & H. Kellerman (Eds.) *Theories of emotion* (pp. 189 -217). New York: Academic Press.

Lee, Y. T., & Seligman, M. E. P. (1997). Are Americans more optimistic than the Chinese? *Personality and Social Psychology Bulletin, 23,* 32-40.

Leibniz, G. W. (1995). R. Ariew and D. Garber. (Eds.) *Philosophical Essays.* Hackett.

Lewin, K. (1935). *A dynamic theory of personality.* New York: McGrawHill.

Loemker, L., (Ed.) (1969). *Leibniz: Philosophical Papers and Letters.* Dordrecht Reidel.

Locke, J. (1975). *Essay concerning human understanding.* Oxford, England: Clarendon Press. (Original work published 1690)

Loewen, J.W. (1996). *Lies My Teacher Told Me: Everything Your American History Textbook Got Wrong.* New York: Touchsotne Books.

Lovallo, D. & Kahneman, D. (2003). Risk and Rationality: Can Normative and Descriptive Analysis Be Reconciled? In Lovallo, D. & Kahneman, D. (Eds.) *Digital Well-Being: Foundations of Hedonic Psychology.* HBR ONLINE

Lykken, D., & Tellegen, A. (1996). Happiness is a stochastic phenomenon. *Psychological Science,* 7, 186-189.

Lyubomirsky, S., Caldwell, N. D., & Nolen-Hoeksema, S. (1998). Effects of ruminative and dis-tracting responses to depressed mood on the retrieval of autobiographical memories. *Journal of Personality and Social Psychology, 75,* 166-177.

Lyubomirsky, S., Kasri, F., & Zebra, K. (2000). Hedonic casualties of self-reflection. Unpublished manuscript, Department of Psychology, University of California. Riverside.

Lyubomirsky, S., & Lepper, H. S. (1999). A measure of subjective happiness: Preliminary reliability and construct validation. *Social Indicators Research, 46,* 137-155.

Lyubomirsky, S., Caldwell, N. D., & Nolen-Hoeksema, S. (1998). Effects of ruminative and distracting responses to depressed mood on the retrieval of autobiographical memories. *Journal of Personality and Social Psychology, 75,* 166-177.

Lyubomirsky, S., & Nolen-Hoeksema, S. (1993). Self-perpetuating propcares of dysphoric rumination. *Journal of Personality and Social Psychology, 65,* 339-349,

Lyubomirsky, S., Caldwell, N. D., & Nolen-Hoeksema, S. (1998). Effects of ruminative and distracting responses to depressed mood on the retrieval of autobiographical memories. *Journal of Personality and Social Psychology, 75,* 166-177.

Lyubomirsky, S., & Nolen-Hoeksema, S. (1995). Effects of self-focused rumination on negative thinking and interpersonal problem solving. *Journal of Personality and Social Psychology, 69,* 176-190.

Lyubomirsky, S., & Lepper, If S. (2000). What are the differences between happiness and self-esteem? Unsubmitted Manuscript.

Lyubomirsky, S., & Nolen-Hoeksema, S. (1993). Self-perpetuating propcares of dysphoric rumination. *Journal of Personality and Social Psychology, 65,* 339-349,

Lyubomirsky, S., & Nolen-Hoeksema, S. (1995). Effects of self-focused rumination on negative thinking and interpersonal problem solving. *Journal of Personality and Social Psychology, 69,* 176-190.

Maier, S. F., & Seligman, M. E. P. (1976): Learned helplessness: Theory and evidence. *Journal of Experimental Psychology: General, 105,* 3-46.

Malouff J.M., Schutte N.S., (Eds.) (1995). Irrational belief scale [IBS] (1986). *Sourcebook of adult assessment.* NY: Plenum Press, pp.432-435

Marks, 1. M., & Nesse, R. M. (1994). Fear and fitness: An evolutionary analysis of anxiety disorders. *Ethology and Sociobiology, 15,* 247-261.

Massimini, F., Csikszentmihalyi, M., & Carli, M. (1987). Optimal experience: A tool for psychiatric rehabilitation. *Journal of Nervous and Mental Disease, 175,* 545-549.

Matthews, D. A., & Larson, D. B. (1997). *The faith factor: An annotated bibliography of clinical research on spiritual subjects* (Vols. I-IV). Rockville, MD: National Institute for Healthcare Research and Georgetown University Press.

McIntosh, D. N., Silver, R. C., & Wortman, C. B. (1993). Religion's role in adjustment to a negative life event: Coping with the loss of a child. *Journal of Personality and Social Psychology, 65,* 812-821.

McFarland, C., & Miller, D. T. (1994). The framing of relative performance feedback: Seeing the glass as half empty or half full. *Journal of Personality and Social Psychology, 66,* 1061-1073.

McGregor, L, & Little, B. R. (1998). Personal projects, happiness, and meaning: On doing well and being yourself. *Journal of Personality and Social Psychology, 74,* 494-512,

McIntosh, D. N., Silver, R. C. & Wormian, C. B. (1993). Religion's role in adjustment to a negative life event: Coping with the loss of a child. *Journal of Personality and Social Psychology, 65,* 812 821.

McCrae, R. R., & Costa, P. T. (1986). Personality, coping, and coping effectiveness in an adult sample. *Journal of Personality, 54,* 385-405.

McCombs, B. (1991). Metacognition and motivation in higher level thinking. Paper presented at the annual meeting of the American Educational Research Association, Chicago, IL.

McCombs, B. & Marzano, R. (2000). What is the role of the will component? In C.E. Weinstein & B.L. McCombs (Eds.), *Strategic learning: Skill, will, and self-regulation.* Hillsdale, NJ: Lawrence Erlbaum Associates.

McFarland, C., & Ross, M. (1982). Impact of causal attributions on affective reactions to success and failure. *Journal of Personality and Social Psychology, 43,* 937-946.

McCrae, R. R., & Costa, P. T. (1986). Personality, coping, and coping effectiveness in an adult sample. *Journal of Personality, 54,* 385-405.

Meyer, D. (1988). *The positive thinkers: Popular religious psychology from Mary Baker Eddy to Norman Vincent Peale and Ronald Reagan* (rev.). Middletown, CT: Wesleyan University Press.

Michalos, A. (1991). *Global report on student well-being: Life satisfaction and happiness.* Vol. 1. New York: Springer-Verlag.

Miller L.J., Feintuch M (2000). Psychiatric disorders in women. *Ob/Gyn Special Edition 47-50.*

Miller LJ: Psychiatric disorders and the menstrual cycle. In Stotland NL, ed., Cutting-Edge Medicine: What Psychiatrists Need to Know. R*eview of Psychiatry, 21.* Washington, DC: American Psychiatric Press, 2002, pp. 113-136

Murray, S. L. (1999). The quest for conviction: Motivated cognition in romantic relationships. *Psychological Inquiry, 10,* 23-34.

Myers, D. G. (1993). *The pursuit of happiness.* New York: Williaim Monow.

Myers, D. G., & Diener, E. (1995). Who is happy? *Psychological Science, 6,* 10-19.

Myers, D. G. (2000). The funds, friends, and faith of happy people. *American Psychologist, 55,* 56-67.

Myers D. (2000) *The American Paradox: Spiritual Hunger in an Age of Plenty* Yale U. Press

Myers, D. Wealth and well-being. (2000). In Stannard, R. (ed.), *God for the 21st Century.* Radnor, PA: Templeton Foundation Press.

Myers, D. G. (1993). *The pursuit of happiness.* New York: Avon.

Myers, D. G., & Diener, E. (1995). Who is happy? *Psychological Science, 6,* 10-19.

Myers, D. G., & Diener, E. (1996, May). The pursuit of happiness. *Scientific American, 274,* 54-56.

211

Myers, D. The funds, friends, and faith of happy people. (2000). *American Psychologist, 55,* 56-67.

Myers, D. Hope and happiness. (2000). In Gillham, J. (ed.), Dimensions of optimism and hope. Radnor, PA: Templeton Foundation Press.

Myers, D. Who is happy? (1995). *Psychological Science, 6,* 10-19. (reprinted in Annual Editions: Social Psychology 97/98.

Myers, D. The pursuit of happiness. (1996, May). Scientific American, pp. 54-56 (by Myers, D. G. & Diener, E.).

Nelson, C. A. (1999). Neural plasticity and human development. *Current Directions in Psychological Science, 8,* 42-45.

Nelson, N. (1988). A meta-analysis of the life-eventlhealth paradigm: The influence of social support. Unpublished doctoral dissertation, Temple University, Philadelphia, Pennsylvania.

Nelson, C. A. (Ed.). (2000). The effects of adversity on neurobehavioral development. Vol. 31. Minnesota Symposia on Child Psychology. Mahwah, NJ: Erlbaum.

Nesse, R. M., & Williams, G. C. (1996). *Evolution and healing: The new science of Darwinian medicine.* London: Phoenix.

Nesse, R. M., & Williams, G. C. (1994). *Why we get sick.* New York: New York Times Books.

Nezu, A. M., Nezu, C. M., & Blissett, S. E. (1988). Sense of humor as a moderator of the relation between stressful events and psychological distress: A prospective analysis. *Journal of Personality and Social Psychology, 54,* 520 525.

Nolen-Hoeksema, S. (1987). Sex differences in unipolar depression: Evidence and theory. *Psychological Bulletin, 101,* 259.

Nolen-Hoeksema, S., Parker, L., & Larson, J. (1994). Ruminative coping with depressed mood following loss. *Journal of Personality and Social Psychology, 67,* 92-104.

Nolen-Hoeksema, S., & Morrow, J. (1991). A prospective study of depression and posstraurnatic stress symptoms after a natural disaster: The 1989 Loma Priem earthquake. *Journal of Personality, and Social Psychology, 61,* 115-121.

Nolen-Hoeksema, S., Parker, L., & Larson, J. (1994). Ruminative coping with depressed mood following loss. *Journal of Personality and Social Psychology, 67,* 92-104.

Oettingen G. (1996). Positive fantasy and motivation. In P. M. Gollwitzer & J. A. Bargh (Eds.), *The psychology of action: Linking cognition and motivation to behavior* (pp. 236-259). New York: Guilford.

Oishi, S., Diener, E., Suh, E., & Lucas, R. E. (1999). The value as a moderator model in subjective well-being. *Journal of Personality, 67,* 157-184,

Okun, M. A., & George, L. K. (1984). Physician- and self-ratings of health, neuroticism and subjective well-being among men and women. Personality and Individual Differences, 5, 533-539.

Okun, M. A., & Stock, W. A. (1987). Correlates and components of subjective well-being among the elderly. *Journal of Applied Gerontology, 6,* 95-112.

Pagels, E. (2003). *Beyond Belief: The Secret Gospel of St. Thomas.* New York: Random House.

Pagels, E. (1989) *The Gnostic Gospels.* New York: Vintage.

Panksepp, J. (1998). Attention deficit hyperactivity disorders, psychostimulants, and intolerance of childhood playfulness: A tragedy in the making? *Current Directions in Psychological Science, 7,* 91-98.

Parducci, A. (1995). *Happiness, pleasure, and judgment: The contextual theory and its applications.* Mahwah, NJ: Erlbaum.

Peterson, C., & Seligman, M. E. P. (1984). Causal explanations as a risk factor for depression: Theory and evidence. *Psychological Review, 91,* 347-374.

Perlman, D., & Rook, K. S. (1987). Social support, social deficits, and the family: Toward the enhancement of well-being. In S. Oskamp (Ed.), *Family processes and problems: Social psychological aspects.* Newbury Park, CA: Sage.

Peterson, C. (2000). The future of optimism. *American Psychologist, 55,* 44-55.

Peterson, C., & Seligman, M. E. P. (1984). Causal explanations as a risk factor for depression: Theory and evidence. *Psychological Review, 91,* 347 374.

Peterson. C., Seligman, M. E. P., & Valliant, G. E. (1988). Pessimistic explanatory style is a risk factor for physical illness: A thirty-five year longitudinal study. *Journal of Personality and Social Psychology, 55,* 23-27.

Peterson, C., Seligman, M. E. P., Yurko, K. H., Martin, L. R., & Friedinan, I. (1998). Catastrophizing and untimely death. *Psychological Science, 9,* 49-52,

Peterson, C. (2000). The future of optimism. *American Psychologist, 55,* 44-55.

Peterson, C. (1988). Explanatory style as a risk factor for illness. *Cognitive Therapy and Research, 12,* 119-132.

Peterson, C. (1991). Meaning and measurement of explanatory style. *Psychological Inquiry, 2,* 1-10.

Peterson, C., & Bossio, L. M. (1991). *Health and optimism.* New York: Free Press.

Peterson, C., Maier, S. F., & Seligman, M. E. P. (1993). Learned helplessness: A theory for the age of personal control. New York: Oxford University Press.

Peterson, C., & Park, C. (1998). Learned helplessness and explanatory style. In D. F. Barone, V. B. Van Hasselt, & M. Hersen (Eds.), *Advanced personality* (pp. 287-3 10). New York: Plenum.

Peterson, C., Schulman, P., Castellon, C., & Seligman, M. E. P. (1992). CAVE: Content analysis of verbatim explanations. In C. P. Smith (Ed.), *Motivation and personality: Handbook of thematic content analysis* (pp. 383-392). New York: Cambridge University Press.

213

Peterson, C., & Seligman, M. E. P. (1984). Causal explanations as a risk factor for depression: Theory and evidence. *Psychological Review, 91,* 347-374.

Peterson, C., Seligman, M. E. P., & Vaillant, G. E. (1988). Pessimistic explanatory style is a risk factor for physical illness: A thirty-five year longitudinal study. *Journal of Personality and Social Psychology, 55,* 23-27.

Peterson, C., Seligman, M. E. P., Yurko, K. H., Martin, L. R., & Friedman, H. S. (1998). Catastrophizing and untimely death. *Psychological Science, 9,* 49-52.

Peterson, C., Semmel, A., von Baeyer, C., Abramson, L. Y., Metalsky, G. I., & Seligman, M. E. P. (1982). *The Attributional Style Questionnaire. Cognitive Therapy and Research, 6,* 287-299.

Peterson, C., & Seligman, M. E. P. (1984). Causal explanations as a risk factor for depression: Theory and evidence. *Psychological Review, 91,* 347-374.

Peterson, K. (1993, October 1). Guys wed for better, wives for worse. *USA Today,* "Life" section, pp. 1-2.

Porges, S. W. (1995). Orienting in a defensive world: Mammalian modifications of our evolutionary heritage: A polyvagal theory. *Psychophysiology, 32,* 301-318.

Porges, S. W. (1995). Orienting in a defensive world: Mammalian modifications of our evolutionary heritage: A polyvagal theory. *Psychophysiology, 32,* 301-318.

Porter, E. H. (1913). *Pollyanna.* London: Harrap.

Price, J. S., & Sloman, L. (1987). Depression as yielding behavior: An animal model based on Schjelderup-Ebb's pecking order. *Ethology and Sociobiology, 8,* 85-98.

Rock, C. L. (2003) Set Point. Personal Communication, USCSD, December, 2003

Ryan, R. M., Sheldon, K. M., Kasser, T., & Deci, E. L. (1996). All goals are not created equal: An organismic perspective on the nature of goals and their regulation. In P. M. Gollwitzer & J. A. Bargh (Eds.),. *The psychology of action: Linking cognition and motivation to behavior* (pp. 7-26). New York: Guilford Press.

Samenow, S. E. (1989) *Before it's too late.* New York: Times Books.

Sax, L. J., Astin, A. W., Kom, W. S., & Mahoney, K. M. (1998). *The American freshman: National norms for fall 1998.* Los Angeles: Higher Education Research Institute, University of California, Los Angeles.

Segrin, C., & Dillard, J. P. (1992). The interactional theory of depression: A meta-analysis of the research literature. *Journal of Social and Clinical Psychology, 11,* 43-70.

Scheier, M. F., & Carver, C. S. (1985). Optimism, coping, and healthAssessment and implications of generalized outcome expectancies, *Health Psychology, 4,* 219-247.

Scheier M. F., & Carver, C. S. (1993). On the power of positive thinking: The benefits of being optimistic. *Current Directions in Psychological Science, 2,* 26-30.

Schmitt, D. P., & Buss, D. M. (1996). Strategic self-promotion and competitor derogation: Sex and context effects on the perceived effectiveness of mate attraction tactics. Journal of Personality and

214

Social Psychology, 70, 1185-1204.

Seeman, T.E., & Berkman, L.F. (1988). Structural characteristics of social networks and their relationship with social support in the elderly: Who provides support. *Social Science and Medicine, 26(7),* 737-749.

Seidlitz, L., & Diener, E. (1993). Memory for positive versus negative life events: Theories for the differences between happy and unhappy persons Journal of Personality and Social Psychology, 64, 654-664.

Seligman, M. E. P., & Csikszentmihalyi, M. (2000). Positive psychology: An introduction. *American Psychologist, 55,* 5-14.

Seligman, M. E. P. (1990). *Learned optimism.* New York: Knopf.

Seligman, M. E. P. (2002). *Authentic happiness.* New York: Simon & Schuster.

Sheehan, N. (1989) *A Bright Shining Lie: John Paul Vann and America in Vietnam.* New York: Vintage.

Sheldon, K. M., & Elliot, A. J. (1999). Goal striving, need-satisfaction, and longitudinal well-being: The Self Concordance Model. *Journal of Personality and Social Psychology. 76,* 482-497.

Sheldon, K. M. (1995). Creativity and goal conflict. *Creativity Research Journal, 8,* 299-306.

Sheldon, K. M., & Emmons, R. A. (1995). Comparing differentiation and integration within personal goal systems. *Personality & Individual Differences, 18,* 39-46.

Sheldon, K. M., & Kasser. T. (1995). Coherence and congruence: Two aspects of personality integration. *Journal of Personality and Social Psychology, 68,* 531 543.

Shenkman, R. (1992). *Legends, Lies, and Cherished Myths of American History.* New York: Perennial.

Shenkman, R.& Reiger, K. (2003) *One-Night Stands with American History: Odd, Amusing, and Little-Known Incidents.*New York: Perennial.

Siegel, J. M., & Kuykendall, D. H. (1990). Loss, widowhood, and psychological distress among the elderly. *Journal of Consulting and Clinical Psychology, 58,* 519-524.

Silver, R. L. (1982). Coping with an undesirable life event: A study of early reactions to physical disability. Unpublished doctoral dissermtion, Northwestern University, Evanston, IL.

Solomon, R. L., & Corbit. J. D. (1974). An opponent-process theory of motivation: 1. Temporal dynamics of affect. *Psychological Review, 81,* 119-145.

Solomon, S., Greenberg, J., & Pyszczynski, T. (1991). A terror management theory of social behavior: The psychological functions of selfesteem and cultural worldviews. *Advances in Experimental Social Psychology, 24,* 93-159.

Somit, A., Christensen & Peterson, S. A. (1996). Indoctrinability as an evolutionary precondition for democracy. *Journal of Social and Evolutionary Systems, 19,* 41-54.

215

Starker, S. (1989). *Oracle at the supermarket: The American preoccupation with self-help books.* New Brunswick, NJ: Transaction.

Staw, B. M., Sutton, R. I., & Pelled, L. H. (1994). Employee positive emotion and favorable outcomes at the workplace. *Organization Science, 5*, 51-71.

Stein, N. L., Folkman, S., Trabasso, T., & Richards, T. A. (1997). Appraisal and goal processes as predictors of psychological well-being in bereaved caregivers. *Journal of Personality and Social Psychology, 72*, 872-884.Strack, F., Argyle, M., & Schwarz, N. (Eds.). (1991). *Subjective wellbeing: An interdisciplinary perspective.* New York: Pergamon Press.

Strack, S., Carver, C. S., & Blaney, P. H. (1987). Predicting successful completion of an aftercare program following treatment for alcoholism: The role of dispositional optimism. *Journal of Personality and Social Psychology, 53*, 579-584.

Studd, M. V. (1996). Sexual harassment. In D. M. Buss & N. M. Malamuth (Eds.), Sex, power, conflict: *Evolutionary andfeministperspectives* (pp. 54-89). New York: Oxford University Press.

Suh, E., Diener, E., & Fujita, F. (1996). Events and subjective well-being: Only recent events matter. *Journal of Personality and Social Psychology, 70*, 1091-1102.

Suh, E., Diener, E., Oishi, S., & Triandis, H. C. (1998). The shifting basis of life satisfaction judgments across cultures: Emotions versus norms. *Journal of Personality and Social Psychology, 74*, 482-493.

Suh, E. M. (2000). Self, the hyphen between culture and subjective well-being. In E. Diener & E. M. Suh (Eds.), Culture and subjective (pp. 63-86). Cambridge, MA: MIT Press.

Symons, D. (1979). *The evolution of human sexuality.* New York: Oxford.

Symons, D. (1987). If we're all Darwinians, what's the fuss about? In C. Crawford, D. Krebs, & M. Smith (Eds.), *Sociobiology and psychology* (pp. 121-145). Hillsdale, NJ: Erlbaum.

Taylor, S. E. (1989). *Positive illusions.* New York: Basic Books.

Taylor. S. E. (1983). Adjustment to threatening events: A theory of cognitive adaptation. *American Psychologist, 38*, 143-49.

Taylor, S. E., & Brown, J. D. (1988). Illusion and well-being: A social psychological perspective on mental health. *Psychological Bulletin, 103*,193-210.

Taylor, S. E., Kemeny, M. E., Reed, G. M., Bower, J. E., & Gmenewald, T. L. (2000). Psychological resources, positive illusions, and health. *American Psychologist, 55*, 99-109.

Taylor. S. E.. & Lobel, M. (1989). Social comparison activity under threat: Downward evaluation and upward contacts. *Psychological Review, 96*, 569-575.

Taylor, S. E., Kemeny, M. E., Reed, G. M., Bower, J. E., & Gmenewald, T. L. (2000). Psychological resources, positive illusions, and health. *American Psychologist, 55*, 99-109.

Tiet, Q. Q., Bird, H. R., Davies, M., Hover, C., Cohen, P., Jensen, P. S., & Goodman, S. (1998). Adverse life events and resilience. *Journal of the American Academy of Child and Adolescent Psychiatry, 37*, 11911200.

Tiger, L. (1979). *Optimism: The biology of hope*. New York: Simon & Schuster.

Tooby. J.. & Cosmides, L. (1990). The past explains the present: Emotional adaptations and the structure of ancestral environments. *Ethology and Sociobiology, 11,* 375-424.

Tooby, J., & Cosmides, L. (1996). Friendship and the banker's paradox: Other pathways to the evolution of adaptations for altruism. *Proceedings of the British Academy, 88,* 119-143.

Trivers, R. L. (1972). Parental investment and sexual selection. In B. Campbell (Ed.), *Sexual selection and the descent of man 1871-1971* (pp. 136-179). Chicago: Aldine.

Tversky. A., & Kahneman, D. (1981). The framing of decisions and the psychology of choice. *Science, 211,* 453-458.

Tversky, A., & Griffin, D. (1991). Endowment and contrast in judgments of well-being. In F. Strack & M. Argyle (Eds.), *Subjective well-being: An interdisciplinary perspective (pp. 10 1- 118).* Oxford, England: Per gamon Press.

U.S. Department of Commerce, Bureau of the Census. (1998). *Statistical abstract of the United States 1996* (116th ed.). Washington, DC: Superintendent of Documents.

Udelman, D. L. (1982). Stress and immunity. *Psychotherapy and Psychosomatics, 37,* 176-184.

de Vattel, E. In Chitty, J. (1883) *Principles of the Law of nature applied to the conduct and affairs of nations and sovereigns*. Philadelphia: TW Johnson & Co.

de Vattel, E. Droit des gens; ou, Principes de la loi naturelle appliqués à la conduite et aux affaires des nations et des souverains (1758; tr. Law of Nations, 1760).

Veenhoven, R. (1988). The utility of happiness. *Social Indicators Research, 20,* 333-354.

Voltaire, F. (1759). *Candide, ou L'Optimisme*. Gen6ve: Cramer.

Weinberger, D., Kolachana B., Fera F., Goldman D., Egan M.F. (2002). Serotonin transporter, genetic variation and the response of the human amygdala. *Science, Jul 19,* 400-432.

Weinstein, N. D. (1989, December 8). Optimistic biases about personal risks. *Science, 246,* 1232-1233
.

Weisse C. S. (1992). Depression and inummocompetence: A review of the literature. *Psychological Bulletin, 111,* 475-489.

Williams. R. B., Barefoot, J. C. & Shekelle, R. B. (1985). The health consequences of hostility. In M. A. Chesney & R. H. Rosenman (Eds.), *Anger and hostility in cardiovascular and behavioral disorders* (pp. 173-185). Washington, DC: Hemisphere.

World Values Study Group. (1994). *World Values Survey, 1981-1994 and 1990-1993* [Computer file, ICPSR version]. Ann Arbor, ME Institute for Social Research.

Williams, R. M., Jr. (1975). Relative deprivation. In L A. Coser (Ed.), *The idea of social construction: Papers in honor of Robert K. Merton* (pp, 355-378). New York: Harcourt Brace Jovairovich.

Williams. R. B., Barefoot, J. C. & Shekelle, R. B. (1985). The health consequences of hostility. In

M. A. Chesney & R. H. Rosenman (Eds.), *Anger and hostility in cardiovascular and behavioral disorders* (pp. 173-185). Washington, DC: Hemisphere.

Williams, R. B., Barefoot, J. C., Califf, R. M., Haney, T. L., Saunders, W. B., Pryor, D. B., Hlatky, M. A., Siegler, 1. C., & Mark, D. B. (1992). Prognostic importance of social and economic resources among medically treated patients with angiographically documented coronary artery disease. *Journal of the American Medical Association, 267,* 520-524.

Winthrop, J. (1965). A model of Christian charity. In E. S. Morgan (Ed.), *Puritan Political Ideas, 1558-1794.* Indianapolis, IN: Bobbs-Merrill. (Original work published 1630)

Wolpe, J. (1958). *Psychotherapy by reciprocal inhibition.* Stanford, CA: Stanford University Press.

Wood, W., Rhodes, N., & Whelan, M. (1989). Sex differences in positive well-being: A consideration of emotional style and marital status. *Psychological Bulletin, 106,* 249-264.

Wood, J. V. (1989). History and research concerning social comparisons of personal attributes. *Psychological Bulletin, 106,* 231 248.

Wright, R. C., & Schneider, S. L. (1999). Motivated self-deception in child molesters. *Journal of Child Sexual Abuse, 8,* 89-111.

Wright, M. O. D., Masten, A. S., Northwood, A., & Hubbard, J. J. (1997) Long-term effects of massive trauma: Developmental and psychobiological perspectives. In Cuchem & S. L. Toth (Eds.), Rochester Symposium on Developmental Psychopathology: Vol 8. *The effects of trauma on the developmental process* (pp. 181-225). Rochester, NY: University of Rochester Press.

Wuthrow R. (1989) *Meaning and Moral Order; Explorations in Cultural Analysis.* San Francisco:UC Press.

Wuthnow, R. (2000). *After Heaven: Spirituality in America Since the 1950s* San Francisco: UC Press.

Zimbardo, P. G. (1985) *Psychology and life,* 11th edition. Glenview, Ill.: Scott, Foresman.

Zinn, H. (2003). *A People's History of the United States 1492-present.* New York: Perennial.

Zinn, H. (2003). *Passionate declarations: Essays on war and justice.* New York: Perennial

Idea and Action Notes

Part I   **The Search for Happiness**

Chapter One   Life, Liberty, the Purchase of Happiness

1. _____
2. _____
3. _____
4. _____
5. _____

Chapter Two   Let Freedom Ring

1. _____
2. _____
3. _____
4. _____
5. _____

Chapter Three   Peace, Order, and Good Government

1. _____
2. _____
3. _____
4. _____
5. _____

Part II   **The Evidence**

Chapter Four   If We're So Rich, Why Are We Miserable?

1. _____
2. _____
3. _____
4. _____
5. _____

Chapter Five   "If It Ain't Broke, Don't Break It"

1. _____
2. _____
3. _____
4. _____
5. _____

Chapter Six   "Maybe If We Moved to California"
1. _____
2. _____
3. _____
4. _____
5. _____

Chapter Seven   Snow White was a Snow Job
1. _____
2. _____
3. _____
4. _____
5. _____

Chapter Eight   War is a Four-Letter Word
1. _____
2. _____
3. _____
4. _____
5. _____

Chapter Nine   Why Be Happy
1. _____
2. _____
3. _____
4. _____
5. _____

Part III   **How to Be Happy**
Chapter Ten   With a Little Help from my Friends
1. _____
2. _____
3. _____
4. _____
5. _____

Chapter Eleven   Happiness: Flow and Faith
1. _____
2. _____
3. _____
4. _____
5. _____

Chapter Twelve   Happiness: The Three Actions:
1. _____
2. _____
3. _____
4. _____
5. _____

Chapter Thirteen   Happiness: The Four Keys:
1. _____
2. _____
3. _____
4. _____
5. _____

Chapter Fourteen   Ubuntu: A Way of Life, a Solution
                          for our World
1. _____
2. _____
3. _____
4. _____
5. _____